11.55

444

3016

THE BIBLE—
AS IF FOR THE FIRST TIME

SPIRITUALITY AND THE CHRISTIAN LIFE
Richard H. Bell, *Editor*

THE BIBLE—
AS IF FOR THE
FIRST TIME

H. A. NIELSEN

THE WESTMINSTER PRESS
Philadelphia

Scripture quotations from the Revised Standard Version of the Bible are copyrighted 1946, 1952, © 1971, 1973 by the Division of Christian Education of the National Council of the Churches of Christ in the U.S.A., and are used by permission.

BOOK DESIGN BY ALICE DERR

First edition

Published by The Westminster Press ®

Philadelphia, Pennsylvania

PRINTED IN THE UNITED STATES OF AMERICA
2 4 6 8 9 7 5 3 1

Library of Congress Cataloging in Publication Data

Nielsen, H. A. (Harry A.)
    The Bible—as if for the first time.

    (Spirituality and the Christian life series)
    Bibliography: p.
    1. Bible—Criticism, interpretation, etc.—Addresses, essays, lectures. 2. Bible—Reading—Addresses, essays, lectures. I. Title. II. Series.
BS540.N53 1984   220.6   83-26053
ISBN 0-664-24612-5 (pbk.)

This book is dedicated to Donna,
who combed many a burr out of its pages

CONTENTS

ACKNOWLEDGMENTS

My thanks to Richard H. Bell for his fine editorial guidance in the writing of this book.

Portions of most of these chapters appeared in print during 1982–83 in *The Canadian Catholic Review*, published monthly in Saskatoon, Saskatchewan, Canada. I am grateful to its editor, Rev. Daniel Callam, C.S.B., for his kind permission to reproduce the material in this volume.

H. A. N.

EDITOR'S INTRODUCTION

In 1609 Francis de Sales published a helpful book designed "to instruct those who live in town, within families, or at court, and by their state of life are obliged to live an ordinary life." It was, as he said, "a collection of bits of good advice stated in plain, intelligible words." The book, *Introduction to the Devout Life*, became a "spiritual classic." Although we will not claim that the books in this series will become spiritual classics, they are intended for a similar reader—one "obliged to live an ordinary life"— and they are written in "plain, intelligible words."

In terms of their subject matter, they share another point with Francis de Sales's book. He said about the Christian life that "a strong, resolute soul can live in the world without being infected by any of its moods." This was not an easy task then, nor is it now. But one of the goals of the Christian life is to free ourselves from circumstances that hinder love and service to God. When the apostle Paul spoke of having the "mind of Christ," he was asking that we not yield to the accidental features of this world; that we strive to free ourselves from being defined by the social, political, and economic contingencies of this world. A great effort of the spirit is needed to do this.

This series is intended to help its readers in this effort

of the spirit. We call these books spiritual because they deal with how God's Spirit intersects with the human spirit. They focus attention on the *Bible* as the principal source for hearing and understanding God's Spirit, and on the *self* as the agent for living in the spirit.

Again, Francis de Sales suggests a strategy that augurs well for the volumes in this series. He asks: "How can we fight against [our imperfections] unless we see them, or overcome them unless we face them?" And he answers: "Our victory does not consist in being unconscious of them but in not consenting to them, and not to consent to them is to be displeased with them." Growth in the spirit involves seeing and facing our imperfections, not consenting to them; it involves being displeased with them and having courage to suffer the wounds meted out by our world. Such growth is given its Christian shape by our memories and stories, by our inner life in its emptiness and fullness, its weakness and strength, as we relate to God as Emmanuel—"God with us." In this concept of *God with us* the series finds its foundation in what is traditionally called *spirituality*.

But more important in this series is how we come to discern God with us and activate our will to make sense of our lives. Thus a second focus is that of building character and its natural outflow in the life of a Christian. The Christian life comes down to how each person faithfully lives in the human community and makes that great effort of spirit in devotion to God and in daily moral and political service.

If no other books you have read lately have encouraged you to take hold of your self and your Christian life with courage and firmness, these books will. They will take you patiently through many identifiable thickets of human life and ask you when it was that you allowed God to speak to you, embrace you, and lead you. These books are intended to be traveling companions, guides to take you closer to the center of the Christian life, closer to the Bible, closer to yourself, and thus, it is hoped, closer to God.

In this book, THE BIBLE—AS IF FOR THE FIRST TIME, H. A. Nielsen devotes attention to the practice of reading the Scriptures alone and for our own sake. "Each of us," he says, "has an open door to the Bible and an invitation to spend some time alone with it." The lessons we learn from responding to this invitation and from taking his tours of the Bible are rich and varied, surprising and refreshing, sobering and eye-opening.

The Bible offers itself as a medium in which one living spirit, that of God the Creator, reaches out to another living spirit, a created human one. In order to activate the biblical texts, the reader has to become active. This requires paying attention to ourselves, to our own responses, as we pay attention to the texts. In this way we draw nourishment for the human spirit. With this personal approach, our reading is much more like a spiritual exercise than a passive experience. It might be said that Nielsen's book is a primer to the more traditional "spirituality"—that which urges more arduous disciplines of the faithful—for his task is simply to get us "to read the Scriptures in a candid, self-involved, conversational way," and that, he notes, "is enormously easier than the religious decision to confess that 'Jesus is Lord' and to stick to it."

There are two hopes for this book, says Nielsen: "The first is that, for some, the Bible will start to look less like a deposit of culture and more like a Promised Land in print, a beckoning estate of fertile lands and waters. The second is that you will see, if you do not see already, that what you have to say to the Bible is just as important as what it has to say to you." We have in this book a fresh way of rediscovering ourselves and the possibility of *God with us* in our encounter with the living Word.

RICHARD H. BELL

PREFACE

Why should a book on how to read the Bible for yourself appear in a series dealing with Christian spirituality?
To answer briefly, there are various ways of reading the
Bible, and not all of them are geared to deliver nourishment to the reader's own spirit or self. Therefore it seemed
in tune with the purpose of this series to devote one volume to the practice of reading the Scriptures alone and for
your own sake. The biblical gate swings open whether
you happen to be a Christian of long standing or an out-
sider looking in. Faith in God and Christ may be the pearl
of great price, but it is not a requirement for reading the
Scriptures on your own.

The Bible is recognized on all sides as a prime foundation stone of Western civilization. A heritage from the
Jewish tradition, it is just as public a property as anything
passed down to us from Athens or Rome. However, the
Bible is also a book that can get acutely personal with you
and me, and can supply meat and drink in ways that are
out of the question for those other ancient inheritances.
The Bible offers itself as a medium in which one living
spirit or self, that of God the Creator, reaches out to another living self, a created human one. In order to activate the biblical texts, the reader has to become active.

This requires paying attention to yourself, to your own responses, as you pay attention to the texts, and entering into two-way communication with them, the closest thing to conversation. One aim of this book is to illustrate that active way of reading by showing what comes of it with a varied selection of texts. Much of what the Bible has to say is said obliquely or indirectly, so a second and related aim of this book is to point to some habits of thought which can enhance the flow of indirect material and thereby make the reading much more like a workout than a passive experience.

Two hopes ride with this book. The first is that, for some, the Bible will start to look less like a deposit of culture and more like a Promised Land in print, a beckoning estate of fertile lands and waters. The second is that you will see, if you do not see already, that what you have to say to the Bible is just as important as what it has to say to you.

H. A. N.

CHAPTER ONE

READING HUMANLY

Here and there in his *Journals*, around the year 1848, the Danish thinker Søren Kierkegaard deplores the fact that scholarly learning about the Bible has so worked its way down to the simplest people that no one can read the Bible in a human way any more. He laments people's loss of the ability to read biblical texts "primitively" or "alone with God," as he puts it. In trying over the years to figure out what reading "primitively" or "humanly" is like, and thus to understand Kierkegaard's hintful but not very concrete expressions, I found it helpful to recall some other ways of reading the Bible. For example, in college just after World War II, one of our textbooks was in fact an edition of the Bible "Designed to Be Read as Living Literature." One way of reading the Bible, then, is to approach it as assigned material in a literature course where you prepare yourself for quizzes about the various story lines, personages, and literary types or "genres." On a second level we find the domain of professional Scripture scholars, ranging from the ultraconservative and orthodox to those thought of as radically "critical" of the Bible. These professionals, too, read the Bible, usually in its original languages and as part of a communal effort to comprehend its historical origins as well as its religious content or message. On a third level we meet persons who approach the Bible as the verbatim revelation of a Deity who demands that people believe every word precisely as written, the hard sayings along with the easy, no questions asked, and that they use it as a sourcebook of answers to life's problems and uncertainties.

The family of meanings of the verb "to read" includes, among others, the three ways of reading the Bible just mentioned. If I understand Kierkegaard's complaint, none of those ways comes close to reading "humanly" or "primitively." Each of the three approaches has its own mind-set and assumptions, and with some justification, for the Bible does wear all three aspects. It is a mighty and reverberant work of letters, an El Dorado for scholars, and—for many—an integral and sufficient revelation, delivering much that we, left to ourselves, could never discover. All three ways, however, share a feature that enables us to set them apart from reading primitively. That is, they all respond to the Bible as to something given, something like a packed basket or hamper that you can carry around and open at will, whereupon it will yield well-wrought literature, knotty problems for researchers, or nuggets of revelation. However, the Bible is too much like another person, an equal or peer, to qualify as a given quantity. One reason is that it contains too much for anyone to possess, even though it is a portable volume. Secondly, like a person, it has depths unplumbed, secrets untold, layers beneath layers, a will and a presence that, taken together, defy any pretense of having it in one's pocket, even if someone with the retentive power of a chess master were to commit the whole thing to memory. In later chapters we will be looking at small sections of biblical material to illustrate these dimensions of Scripture.

Here at the start, however, we may observe that when someone reads it primitively, the Bible is never something well in hand, never something whose limits and stable disposition one can safely take for granted. This is most evident where a text puts its readers under siege—for instance, by calling them transgressors from the moment of their birth. Here the text generates a poser: "How can such a saying conceivably apply to me?" If the Bible contains hints to a solution, there remains the task of winkling them out and piecing them together. Until this effort has been made, there is not much sense in the reader's claiming to have the doctrine well in hand, or to understand the text, or even to believe it without understanding.

More specifically, "reading primitively" means, first of all, reading as a creature who has other things to do and to think about, so that one cannot live immersed in the Scriptures. This makes for selective reading, and the principle of selection is the reader's constant (if sometimes back-burner) awareness of personal needs. The Bible makes us heirs and heiresses to an estate, the grounds of which are too immense to survey with the unaided eye, and we have to acquaint ourselves with its numerous features and sites by taking informal walks in it. These walks do not constitute research by any scholarly standard, nor need they. Their purpose is to put us in touch with individuals whose needs parallel our own. If I have discovered, for example, that my interior life is in a state of arrested growth, or that I can't shake off my hard feelings about having been shortchanged in some aspect of my life, or that I have gotten myself trapped in a situation with no clear avenue of escape, then I know in a general way what sort of parallel to look for.

Our personal needs are various and often blend into one another. Sometimes I need basic nourishment and water; at other times stimulation, courage, a reminder, a clue, a show of affection, a trail blazed by someone else, a bath, a warning, a little recognition, a jolt, some amusement, a shift of perspective, a place to hide. A creature with personal needs like these must, if they are to be met, move into the Scriptures at ground level where the rains bring forth corn and the small springs bubble—and at ground level the field of vision is quite limited. However, there may be other occasions when the nonpersonal needs of the scholarly community require someone to make aerial reconnaissance over larger portions of the scriptural territory, but always with the understanding that that person too has primitive needs and must touch down from time to time to satisfy them. This means, for example, that when reading primitively one reads in the language one knows best, that in which one's personal needs find their most finely shaded expression, even if one is versed in Hebrew and Greek.

Approaching the Bible with an awareness of one's personal needs, whether they be acute or unpressing at the time, does not make a reader any less a member of whatever communities he or she happens to be involved with, but it helps develop a technique of reading that is adapted to extracting the personal nourishment and light contained in the Scriptures, as later chapters will illustrate. When I turn to the Bible as a rumored source of enlightenment and help for my own needs as a person, I can set aside the special needs of the theological community or the scholarly community. The rumor of nourishment is my passport into the Scriptures, and if there are profound problems about the inspiration, authority, and revelatory character of the Bible, or about the existence and essence of God, then—for the time being at least—they are not my problems but those of the aforementioned communities.

A prime personal need that the Bible can help to satisfy is the need to know myself better. Self-knowledge is a layered notion, and one of its layers is concerned with the familiar business of "getting wise to myself" or becoming aware of my strengths and gifts as well as my wiles, my get-away-with-it mentality, or my affinity for paths of least resistance. The Bible overlaps with human wisdom in offering examples. Another equally important layer of self-knowledge concerns the task of investigating for myself to see if my life actually contains certain complications that the Bible repeatedly alludes to. Am I in fact in a state of mutiny or revolt? Do I in fact nurse in myself the longing for and expectation of an eternal joy? Can I adjust myself to the rumor that a divine Maker took pity on me? Can I be happy with the thought that someone can see right through me? And, where these questions place me in a conflict-of-interest situation, can I trust my first answers?

If the rule in reading primitively is to enter into the Scriptures at ground level and on foot, it goes without saying that the reader had better travel light, leaving behind the high-powered lighting equipment and special lenses, coated against glare, that may be indispensable to other ways of reading the Bible. To read humanly is to read with our natural organ of sight, the naked eye, which can sometimes be dazzled and also now and then find that it is completely in the dark. The naked eye is a primary spotter of texts that bear upon the personal needs just mentioned. This point is easily misunderstood, for it might be taken as suggesting that in order to read humanly I have to become a sort of actor and project my mentality back into a state of childlike naiveté and ignorance, blotting out anything I might know about science. Must I in fact split my mind down the middle and seal off objective knowledge of the laws of physics, of how many billion years old the earth is, and similar things, in order to fake a childlike attitude? Not at all. In the first place, the Bible confronts its readers with material no child can handle. The child can read humanly, but can handle only childish material. If an adult goes up to the Bible with those personal needs never out of sight, the scientific knowledge he or she happens to possess will normally have no role to play in the primitive interview, nor will there be any need to fake an attitude. These last points will become clearer when we look closely at the biblical passages up ahead.

Material extraneous to the Bible can interfere with effective solo reading in any number of ways. For example, it is highly unhelpful to assign a genre name such as "history," "theology," "myth," "poetry," "didactic fiction," or "inerrant Word of God" to any section of the Bible. By placing the opening chapters of Genesis in the genre "creation myths," for instance, I group those chapters with a sizable class of documents, which means I am implicitly likening the Genesis material to other things that are generally understood to be myths. There may indeed be obvious resemblances between Genesis and, say, the Babylonian stories of creation, in that both speak of the beginnings of the world and humans, and even employ similar forms of expression. However, to read Genesis as a document of a certain genre amounts to reading it with less than full attention, for the other accounts of creation cry out for equal time on the basis of resemblances that may be quite superficial. This pretty well guarantees that Genesis will not unload any surprises on me that would place it in a class by itself (for instance, basic instruction in the use of the word "God"), since my expectations as I approach the text are not primitively open but are controlled by the classification "creation myth." I thus allow only those wavelengths appropriate to creation myths to get through to me; if it should happen that the surface-level narrative is a vehicle for other kinds of instruction (linguistic, ethical, or whatever), those other messages will very likely be lost or scrambled.

Even the most low-grade extraneous material can get in the way of candid conversation between a reader and the Gospels. For example, it is practically a truism in many minds that, compared with the more historical Synoptic Gospels, the Gospel of John is laced with developed theology. If I bring this judgment (whether it is true or not) to a reading of John, it equips me with an overview of all four Gospels based on someone's comparison. However, to be comparing Gospels in this or that respect, a task that is certainly in order for an exegete or Scripture scholar, places me already at too wide a distance for intimate conversation, whispers and all, and takes in far more terrain than a naked pair of eyes can keep in focus at ground level. Similarly, the scholarly distinctions "Synoptics/ John" and "historical/theological" can modify my cast of mind by leading me to imagine I know something about John the Evangelist: he spikes his history with headier stuff. Inevitably this will tend to make my conversation with John's Gospel a guarded one.

Reading for personal nourishment implies a readiness to let a biblical text speak its piece in full, at least for openers, and along with this a readiness on the reader's part to express any personal bafflement, confusion, uncertainty, wonderment, amazement, hard feelings, or any other state of mind that the text happens to generate. These expressions are common in informal conversation and often are instrumental in moving it forward. To return to an earlier example, it is unsettling and confusing to be told that I was born in rebellion against God, that I am a born rebel (Isa. 48:8, for example), and there are natural moves one makes to quiet the unsettlement and reduce the confusion. These include searching out other parts of the Scriptures that might shed light on the biblical idea of *inherited* sin, which is different enough from other applications of the word "sin" to require some effort on my part in order to see how, if at all, it could pertain to me. However, suppose some readers have become convinced, on whatever grounds, that the idea of inherited sin is incoherent, a relic of a bygone age when people were less clearheaded than they are today. For those readers no personal disturbance or confusion will arise when they encounter that charge in the Bible, since they are in a certain sense protected from its sting by having a ready-made category such as "incoherent relic" in which to place any biblical assertion about them that resists immediate penetration. Because they have preclassified the charge of inherited sin as something other than a shot fired across their own bow, they will see no point in looking further to see how it might apply to themselves.

In such ways, then, extraneous material can block the give-and-take of conversation by altering our perspective, distancing us from the text, or shielding us from its immediate personal impact. When this happens we forfeit the chance to express our own initial response to the text, which would have made a bridge to further conversation. The idea of a conversation developing stage by stage hints at something odd about how the Bible puts itself across in a primitive reading. First of all, it addresses its readers on their home ground, presupposing that they are human beings—risking a reader's hauteur or a cold shoulder in case the reader is something over and above that, such as a star athlete or a poet laureate. Secondly, the Bible will deliver a seemingly outrageous line, declaring, for example, that I have been born one time too few. This is enough to launch a conversation, provided I respond, even if all I can think of is: "I don't understand a word of that" or "What on earth could that mean?" Just as in ordinary conversation we often ask for a clarification of the other's opening remark, so I can ask the Bible to clarify a puzzling overture.

This does not mean, however, that the Bible will answer as a human companion often does, with a clarifying gloss or paraphrase or with a parcel of language that looks tailored to my query. More often than not it replies obliquely, and one way of doing this is by the use of living examples. If I can't make head or tail of an alleged need to be born anew, the reason may be that language has reached an outer limit here and the understanding has to shift gears into another form of expression, where paraphrase, no longer helpful, gives way to a more ostensive technique. That is, I have to look at some individuals to whom the Bible applies the concept "born anew" and who apply it to themselves. The most obvious examples are Peter, Paul, Stephen, and other personages in The Acts of the Apostles. I can augment my grasp of the concept "second birth" by noting how these people conducted themselves, what others thought of them, what they allowed themselves to be put through, and how they behaved at death's door.

There is a cowpath, then, leading to that text from baffling Gospel references to a second birth, and other crooked paths pick up from there to guide inquirers who turn to the Bible with their own needs centrally in mind. Here I choose the rustic term "cowpath" to help distinguish the route of solo readers from the much broader avenue of historical scholarship where many can march abreast—but march with communal rather than personal questions uppermost, and with a communal understanding and method. "Primitive" readers, too, seek to satisfy their understanding (of the concept "second birth," for example), but by means of a different sort of excursion into the Scriptures, with all heavy equipment left behind. This is not because they disdain the methods and apparatus of scholarship; in fact, from nine to five they may be professional Scripture scholars, doing their primitive reading after hours. No, it is because they want answers to questions dealing with their own lives that they travel the cowpaths on foot, knowing full well that for other kinds of concerns their scholarly books and journals are indispensable.

In following the cowpaths from a baffling text to other texts that shed a little light on it, the individual reader bumps into unsearchable or scientifically baffling episodes—for example, the account of the Apostles making themselves understood to foreigners who speak a dozen different tongues, in Acts 2. Getting across to people in languages I haven't learned is something I cannot manage, but this becomes instructive in itself concerning the dark concept of inherited sin. I can now begin to associate sin with certain human incapacities that up to now I have regarded as "natural," such as my inability to communicate well with persons who speak only Finnish or Armenian. This is far from a complete understanding of inherited sin as it relates to me, but by connecting it to obvious inabilities of my own, with the help of a contrast supplied by Acts 2, I have made a beginning.

When someone reads it humanly, the Bible can do something that the mainline churches find more and more difficult to do. That is, it can help an individual to perceive Christianity as if for the first time, much as if the sudden and startling eruption that it originally created had occurred in our own day. Sharpening one's awareness of what Christianity is amounts merely to clearing one's vision and should not be likened to becoming a Christian or to what Christians call spiritual growth. It is related, however, to growth of the spirit insofar as it enables an individual to locate, extract, and use for his or her personal needs the Bible's nourishment, oxygen, and light by taking a more active role in the reading process. As the ability to read actively develops or, for some individuals, restores itself, the person acquires more confident command of biblical concepts, such as "God," "spirit," and "revelation," that are initially quite opaque. Problems about the inspiration and authority of the Testaments gradually lose their power to vex when in the flow of conversation with biblical texts the active reader can perceive those elements for himself or herself, though only indirectly—for example, in the extraordinary things that the biblical authors do with language. Even the ancient problem "Does God exist?" dries up. Under active reading, what looks like a dry crust of text often reveals underlayers of content that turn it into a full-course meal.

Faith is not required in order to read the Bible actively. The road is just as open to nonbelievers as to believers, which is not to say, of course, that their reading experiences will be identical, though they will overlap. For the most part these will not be *religious* experiences, and certainly not the raptures and ecstasies of the mystics. It does not require conversion or faith or a religious commitment to experience astonishment, for example, at the way language is made to perform in certain Gospel narratives, and any respectable translation will do for this purpose. In order to discover and appreciate what the Bible contains, all that is required of the adult reader is *to keep the lines of two-way communication open.* This is not a guarantee of optimal spiritual growth, but is an important condition for it.

A dread of reading humanly, a fear that one might come away believing too much, is real in many minds. But what does it mean to *believe* that someone cleansed ten lepers in a flash or walked on water? Does it mean anything more than that I let myself take part in the conversations that these narratives touch off? For that may be all I can do with a particular narrative. The inscrutable elements in the Bible are often the conversation pieces that start an exchange going because they hook up with my personal needs and questions. Even if leprosy is rare these days and drownings are uncommon, are there not countless kinds of unclearness and countless ways of drowning? It is mind-numbing to be told that these events took place, but if the function of the baffling narratives is precisely to baffle, and thus to engage an active reader in close conversation, then that function at any rate is clear enough, even if I never get clear about how to walk on the waves.

The Christian church, which originally assembled the

New Testament and bound it to the Old, has since become divided and in many respects less trumpet-tongued than the ancient Scriptures, especially in matters of terminology. Controversies over definitions and fine shades of doctrine may be highly important, but they form no part of an active reader's interviews with the Bible. He or she does not bring to those interviews the priorities of a church or of the scholarly community, but rather the priorities of a creature who is given only one shot at existence and who experiences personal needs.

There is one last, practical word for the active reader: As you go through the rest of this book it would be a good idea to familiarize yourself with the section of biblical material discussed in each chapter, and to keep it at hand to refresh your memory of the details.

CHAPTER TWO

GENESIS:
LAYERS AND SILENCES

If you approach the Bible as a solo reader and in a way that leaves you open to surprises, you will get surprises, not necessarily on every page, but often enough to keep you coming back for more. Assuming, of course, that you don't mind surprises. Not all surprises are agreeable, as we know from bee stings and speed traps. In the opening chapters of Genesis, however, we find the kind of surprise that comes when you look at a familiar text for the hundredth time, and this time a veil is lifted, a mist dissolves, and for a while you can only look on in amazement at the way the language of the text has been managed before your eyes, the way the biblical language *acts*, the things the biblical author does with it and does to the reader with it.

Part of keeping yourself open to the unexpected when you read alone and for yourself is remembering your personal needs as you read. Secondly, even if you know more than one language, read for yourself in the language you think about your troubles in. Finally, don't try to control what the Bible is allowed to say to you, and don't hold back your spontaneous responses and questions. The advantage of reading by yourself is that you can stop anywhere to have your say or let a bit of text sink in. In church, contrastingly, there is always the next reading or the next hymn or whatever the pastor has in mind.

By sitting down alone with the first two chapters of the book of Genesis, you can sample the biblical kind of truth and freedom just in those opening pages. Reading for yourself, however, means first putting out of mind everything you may have read or heard *about* those chapters. To begin with, avoid assigning any literary form to what you are going to read. Don't think of it as story, folklore, creation myth, saga, metaphor, or symbolism, or as the poetic effort of an ancient people to understand itself. Classifying it by literary form raises expectations that can interfere with a personal reading and conceal the surprises. If your Bible has footnotes, ignore them—this time. If you own a commentary on Genesis, keep it out of sight for this reading. Forget also, if you can, that there is a famous, noisy theory that ventures a scientific picture of human origins. Try to think of those two chapters as a piece of mail you haven't opened yet. You don't even recognize the handwriting on the envelope. It may take some practice, but by clearing your mind of outside voices, you can manage to be alone with the text. Now let it speak, for by distancing yourself for an hour from rumors and opinions about it, you have freed it to speak.

What do those short chapters tell you concerning, for instance, how humans came to be on earth? They convey right on the surface that a lordly mentality oversaw the making of all that was made, men and women included and crowning the list. But this is not exactly an answer to the question "How?" The text says that God breathed life into something formed of dust and slime; anyone who thinks that this tells us *how* humankind came into existence should mingle some dust and slime and try breathing life into it. Nobody has the dimmest idea of how to bring dust to life or fashion a woman out of a bone. Our understanding soon runs aground if we try to make out the "how" from details about Adam's rib. Those details belong to the *letter* of the text. Let your reading flow around the opaque details, then, in order not to get snagged on the letter, and when you come to the end of ch. 2 look back at them. What do they tell you?

It may come as a surprise to someone reading in this way, alone and with the naked eye, that those chapters tell nothing at all about how the human race began. We come away empty on that question. The details, which at first glance give the appearance of telling us the "how" of it, only reveal our ignorance as soon as we try to fathom the creative process. You have to try to fathom it and watch yourself fail at the attempt in order to notice this part of the message: namely, that you remain in the dark about how our kind got started. At this point we begin to catch the *spirit* of the text, not the letter, and the spirit begins by reminding the individual of a personal darkness, ignorance, unknowing. The mighty intelligence that according to Genesis formed the first humans, and that formed us too, keeps silent about the "how."

By going this far with the first two chapters, you are reminded of a truth about yourself: you don't know what creative and sustaining powers it takes to hold a human life together, whether Adam's or yours. It is up to you, though, to *taste* this truth by admitting it personally: "I am under no illusions about understanding this," or words to that effect. It is a sign that you have gotten into the spirit of the text whenever it gets personal. The letter of the text, on the other hand, speaks of dust or a rib or other people and does not get personal.

This meager, slightly humbling personal truth is one that many today do not like the taste of and cannot bring themselves to admit. They are convinced that science has cracked the riddle of human origins or will soon break the inside story. But it should not be difficult for a candid reader to admit personal ignorance of the powers needed to put together a race of creatures with language, freedom, and personality. If you admit that patch of ignorance, awareness of it will keep you teachable, keep you open to layer after layer of instruction in those two short chapters alone, not to mention the vast remainder of the Bible.

Having tasted truth in the words of your own admission, you can go on to taste the freedom those chapters bestow on anyone who reads them actively—for example, the personal freedom to *wonder*. We count our blessings in this part of the world, aware of countries where personal freedoms have been cut to the bone by police states, totalitarian regimes, dictatorships. But a very great number of our own people are in a sort of police state of mind in this free land. They have lost a personal freedom, the freedom to wonder about the human race, one's own part in it, what ultimately sustains it, where it is headed, and similar things. They cannot wonder because they have been told that science has pretty well answered those questions, and that if they want to know the details they can look them up in any library. In short, many people have picked up the habit, from news media and books, of regarding human evolution as known beyond a doubt. Their original ignorance, the spark plug of wonder, won't spark any more, since there isn't much point in wondering if you think you already know. The opening chapters of Genesis, on the other hand, declare to anyone who listens with a personal ear, "You are ignorant of these matters, so feel free to wonder."

Have you held on to your original ability to wonder? Can you *taste* the wonder? When you acknowledge your ignorance and thus spark the wonder, you can taste it by venting it in your own words, by giving it personal expression. "Here I am, the only kind of creature on earth that can think and speak and learn and know things. Why am I in the dark about the deepest roots of my life and the life of the global human family?" But your own words will have a stronger taste than these. "Bring your wonder to me with no strings attached," says the Bible, "and I will give you something for it. I will not put your wonder under arrest as humans often do, but will let it lead you deeper into the Word of the Most High, for on this opening page or two I have given you only a lick of truth and a lick of freedom." Only a foretaste?

Then let us look again, this time confining ourselves to the first chapter.

Chapter 1 of Genesis looks enough like other ancient Middle Eastern accounts of creation to tempt some to regard it as a myth, one more story about the doings of a deity. Yet Genesis 1 is anti-myth. It puts out of office all the mythical gods and goddesses of light and darkness, sea and sky, plant life and crops and harvest, sun and moon, the animal world, and—finally—human affairs. The text wages a six-day war against myths, all the while looking more or less like a myth. This requires a certain ability to manage the languages of humans, and all of them at once, for it scarcely matters for this anti-myth effect which translation you read.

We notice a layer that hints at the kind of being God is. Half a dozen times God pauses, steps back, and observes that the things he made are very good. This gesture is something we humans do now and then in our workplaces, kitchens, studios, and so forth, and much can be gathered from it. You can gather, for example, that God is mindful of everything he made, that he is independent of all of it, and that he is not troubled by shortages of anything. There is nothing new in these teachings, all of them rooted far back in Judaism. Your own life expresses belief in them, for example, whenever you spontaneously like or admire a scene or a creature not made by human hands, such as great waves rolling ashore or a jewel-like beetle.

Perhaps the most profound imprint of those teachings

is on our habits of speech. We guard our tongues against doing them violence. Traditions of great antiquity stand in the way of our saying that the world is the outcome of mindless forces, or that humankind is the chance by-product of a blind cosmic process, or that historical events are beyond God's control. In the main we let the teachings keep our thinking within their broad fairways and out of the rough. And when we find ourselves inclined, perhaps in a bleak mood, to drift toward hostile ideas, our will comes into play and brings us back to those teachings.

Why would free and self-reliant adults let their speech, thought, even their will, be shaped, or partly shaped, by a cluster of teachings that go back so far in time? If human tyrants set out to make our speech, thought, and will conform to their own, people would resist mightily. Regimes exist today that stifle speech, police the citizen's thoughts, and seek to bend or break the human will. The mere idea of other humans setting out to produce such conformity, whether by issuing decrees, putting chemicals in the water, or using secret police would strike us as monstrous. No human has, or should have, such authority over another.

But the teachings in Genesis 1 let us be ourselves. The pressure is there, gently forming our minds around those teachings, yet no one thinks of Genesis 1 as enslaving or oppressive. Even people who regard it as a myth, which is a common misunderstanding, see it as majestic and uplifting. The teachings let us be ourselves, yet at the same time they steadily push the mind in a direction it would not take of its own accord.

Something remarkable, something unexpected, begins to make itself felt after you spend some time alone with that opening chapter. The remarkable thing shows itself first of all in the layered texture. The top layer, as we saw earlier, reminds one of a personal ignorance by conveying what seems to be information. A second layer leads us away from mythologies while it mimics a myth. A third proposes to channel and restrict our speech and thought, but without putting a damper on freedom and personality. All of these half-veiled communications occur in a single chapter consisting of thirty-one short verses. If you have ever wondered what people mean when they speak of "the living word," you can make some sense of the phrase by reflecting on your experience as an active reader. When you open the book to Genesis 1, the printed words look ordinary enough. This changes as soon as you start paying attention to yourself along with the text. Then the text becomes animated, spirited. It becomes personal. This is a sign of life, something that only a living spirit can manifest. The signs of life in the Word confront you in response to your own signs of life, such as paying attention and refusing to get stuck on the letter of the text.

The remarkable thing, viewed from another angle, is the power to make simple sentences perform so many athletic functions in one small chapter. Genesis 1, when read actively, proves to be an uncommonly crafted piece of writing. The ability to communicate on those several levels, using only the words of ordinary speech, shows a mastery of literary technique almost beyond belief. We often say of excellent writers that they write "with authority," and in Genesis 1 we see such authority unsurpassed. True, the magnificence is veiled. It wears the dusty mask of an ancient document. But when you look at *what* it communicates, and *how* it does so, Genesis 1 is as fresh as if it had been written this morning.

Now is a good time to read Genesis 3, which in its filmy way accounts for our ignorance. It tells us that man and woman in collusion lost or threw away the right to know their source. Human origins remain swathed in mist for a reason, and this might be a biblical hint that science will not get very far with the question, despite all the media hubbub about "man's ancestors." However, we find that those three chapters pay off in another kind of coin, if we count our change carefully. They give us a particular concept of ourselves, of humankind, of the human race. It is not the only possible way to conceive of ourselves, and many people today think they know a better way, but since it is sustained all through the Bible we have reason to view it as God's conception of us.

The gist of God's idea of humankind is that we form a network of relatives—mothers, sons, uncles, grandparents, and so forth—some of them close, others distant, but all stemming from the same root. Born into the protective network, each of us, helpless at first, slowly comes of age in the supportive nests where we learn how to speak, how to listen, and how to manage our budding freedom. Each of us comes into the world at a disadvantage, yet as an equal of the older, more advantaged ones. How an equal? Well, relatives are equals, and each of us comes into existence as a relative, a son or daughter, a sibling, and a grandchild. The adults can see themselves in the speechless infant; they can remember the infant in themselves. The network assures a firm, well-defined place for whoever comes along. No new arrival is nameless or just extra, and none comes as a surprise to God.

The human *family*, then, is a landmark concept in the Bible. Countless passages reinforce it in the most varied ways. For example, we are all descendants of the family of Noah (Genesis 6–9), as was Abraham:

> The Lord appeared to Abram, and said, "To your descendants I will give this land." (Gen. 12:7)

In all the columns of "begats" before and after the covenant with Abraham, each name stands firm in its niche between two generations. "Honor your father and your

mother," God commands in Exodus 20. In the hymnbook
of Zion the psalmist puts the same theme in another key:

> For thou didst form my inward parts,
> 　thou didst knit me together in my mother's
> 　womb.
> I praise thee, for thou art fearful and wonder-
> 　ful.
> Wonderful are thy works!
> Thou knowest me right well;
> 　my frame was not hidden from thee,
> when I was being made in secret,
> 　intricately wrought in the depths of the earth.
> 　　　　　　　　　　　　(Ps. 139:13–15)

Prophets, too, sound that theme. Through the lips of
Isaiah, the Lord speaks to Israel, whose ups and downs
parallel those of the individual:

> But Zion said, "The LORD has forsaken me,
> 　my Lord has forgotten me."
> "Can a woman forget her sucking child,
> 　that she should have no compassion on the
> 　son of her womb?
> Even these may forget,
> 　yet I will not forget you.
> Behold, I have graven you on the palms of my
> 　hands."
> 　　　　　　　　　　　　(Isa. 49:14–16)

The motif runs again through the New Testament, for
example in Luke 1:

> The angel said to her, "Do not be afraid, Mary,
> for you have found favor with God. And be-
> hold, you will conceive in your womb and bear
> a son, and you shall call his name Jesus. He will
> be great, and will be called the Son of the Most
> High." (Luke 1:30–32)

Explicitly you and I are told that we are distinct and

once-only creations, that we are not retreads or replicas but recent arrivals. "Remember also your Creator in the days of your youth" (Eccl. 12:1). May the new grandchild, too, come of age and remember. If each one is an original, separately conceived and endowed with existence, moral consequences flow from this which are not so easy to extract from a Big Bang picture of a mindless universe. For example, no one of our kind, and no one turning into one of our kind, is a throwaway or just extra. The fact that in our time various circles turn a cold shoulder to this teaching is reason enough for reminding ourselves of it.

Inexhaustibly, then, Creation keeps coming at us. How, though, can I train myself to perceive the new *as* new and not merely as a weary cyclical repetition? For that purpose I must never let go of my own small human mentality, or merge it so completely with a corporate one that it can't raise a personal shout of welcome when it perceives the new. Your mentality and mine can tell when something is new, even when, to another sort of mind, it looks like a rehash of the same old thing.

CHAPTER THREE

HOW A GOSPEL COMMUNICATES

The account in Mark 6:45–52 is, on the face of it, a "turbulence account" like most—though not quite all—of the narratives in the Gospels. Those narratives speak of turbulence in private lives, in official circles both Jewish and Roman, in urban and rural settings, in sea and sky, occasionally even in sealed tombs. For the most part the evangelists let the moments of turbulence speak for themselves. How then does this moment of turbulence, of a man walking on water, speak?

Start with the most elementary aspect of the text, its immediate content. While the spectacle might not disturb the rhythm of a cow's chewing, a man walking on water is doing something humans can't do, and the disciples in the boat, Mark tells us, are baffled, terrified. No one needs faith to grasp that a walker on the waves, no matter how like us the person might be, is in that respect as unlike us as a bug scooting on the surface of a pond. If you are reading the text for yourself and for the nourishment it offers, then on this occasion you will let no one come between you and the text, not even the most learned or the saintliest person. You will not imagine that it is your task to investigate how such an account got into the New Testament, or to make judgments about its credentials like a treasury official checking for counterfeit coins. Your task for the present is not to do the talking but to let the text speak to you. Once it speaks, you are free to answer and to raise questions, but these will be *original* questions. They will originate in your own mind, in one person's mind, and not in the corporate mind either of a community of scholars or of the church.

For example, an enormous difference strikes the human eye when it confronts the immediate content of Mark 6. A solo reader might well puzzle over it and ask, "Have I got even a *name* for the difference between me and someone who can do what humans can't do?" If a name for that difference is not too much to ask, where would a reader look for it except in the same source where the narrative occurs? As it happens, if we look further we do in fact find a name for the difference in quite a few places: sin. It is not the most fathomable word in the world or the most fashionable, but it keeps turning up.

Now a curious twist begins to appear. The difference, the sole difference, between the walker on the waves and you or me is called *sin*. But then, am I being told that except for sin, I too could walk on water and do the other things in Mark 6 that humans can't do, multiply loaves of bread and kill armies of germs with my bare hands? The fact of the matter is, I have no well-formed idea of what I could do if it were not for sin, no clear idea of what power sources, if any, I could tap into at will except for sin. And while we are on the subject, what is sin? By putting our earlier question to Mark 6, we seem to be led to a sense of the term "sin" that points beyond what people the world over call sins or evildoings. It points to a condition that embraces every aspect of a person's existence, but a condition you can't detect however closely you inspect yourself. Particular sins are something we can discover, plan, consciously commit, later recall, and so forth. However, a stain that permeated the whole of my existence could not be thought, could not for example be discovered by hard thinking, since my thinking capacity along with the rest of me would be dyed with the same dye.

If every human were in fact in such an unthinkable, all-enveloping state, how would anyone ever become aware of it? As we keep that question in mind, the curious twist I spoke of appears in this way: Underneath the *immediate* content of Mark 6 lies a further content that comes to light as I let the immediate lead me into conversation with other parts of the book. What we shall call a *mediate* (indirect) content comes into view: a sin message, hints of an unperceivable state that holds me fast. In Mark 6 this mediate content reveals my state by means of a contrast with someone who is not in that state, a sinless one, as other texts in the New Testament assert directly. Who would have imagined that a man walking on water would call to mind an unthinkable condition in the rest of us instead of just in himself? Who would have surmised that such a condition is what makes water wings a must for children at the beach? We have no secular basis for connecting the fact that we can drown with anything that lies beyond the reach of thought or human discovery or science.

Mark 6 makes no mention of sin. This suggests that one function of its language is to uncover and impart an indirect message by drawing an individual, such as you or me, into a conversation touched off by the direct content. And drawing very gently—for if I am in a state repellent to whatever powers made me, no doubt those powers could really rub my nose in it by, for example, making me hideous to myself. But instead a man walks on the waves, and sin is not mentioned. The presence of an indirect content helps explain why so many searching minds over the centuries have experienced no difficulty ingesting a text such as Mark 6, despite its stubborn opaqueness. Normally, that is, people are positioned to receive indirect material along with the direct. This is not to suggest, of course, that the mind of every solo reader operates in precisely the sequence just described. However, the average reader does not start from the hard-line premise that the Gospels communicate directly and in no other way; consequently a number of difficulties that critical scholarship finds in the surface layer of a text such as Mark 6 strike the ordinary reader as trouble free.

So far nothing like *faith* is involved in these remarks, but only (*a*) reading an account of some local turbulence, (*b*) noticing the immediate content, (*c*) observing that it alludes to a sharp difference between me and the walker on the waves, (*d*) tracking down a name for the difference, and (*e*) allowing a mediate or indirect content to unfold. Merely being made somewhat aware of an unthinkable state is a long way from putting it behind me, repenting, receiving faith, or however one chooses to express it. "But you couldn't get this far in your colloquy with the Gospel," someone objects, "unless you did more than *read* that someone walked on the water. You also have to *believe* that he did so, and despite your disclaimer this means you bring *faith* into your reading." It is worth a pause to examine the misunderstanding here. What does the objector mean by *believing* the account? Actually one can do very little with an account of a hopelessly baffling performance other than put baffled questions to it, such as "How come he can do that but I can't?" I cannot prove or disprove that the event happened; I can't retell it in clear historical prose, since it contains a baffling element; nor can I repeat the performance. The most I can do is let the text take me by the hand and lead me, via my own queries, to other texts that happen to be present in the same source and happen to say something unexpected about my state. The objector has confused *believing* the text with *giving it a hearing*. Giving it a hearing means letting it unfold its indirect content in response to my questions, since its direct content is as much of a puzzlement to me as Mark says it was to the men in the boat.

From what we have noted it would appear that *reading* the text for myself, as opposed to scanning it or studying it scientifically, requires of me that I *do not choke off the flow of indirect content*. I dare not assume that the immediate content conveys all that the text has to say. Where that assumption prevails, a staid reader will see the account of Jesus walking on water as religious foolishness or myth in a damaging sense, while a more pliant reader will see it as ecstatic overstatement, poetry, metaphor, or myth in a softer sense. Inevitably the text will withhold its indirect payload from any reader who works under that assumption.

To summarize, the language of Mark 6 works by first presenting a turbulence account containing a baffling element, which in turn has a function: it apprises readers of a so-far nameless difference between themselves and the walker on the waves. By allowing this to lead or draw them into other corners of the New Testament, they become aware of an indirect disclosure of their own condition back in Mark 6. This disclosure takes place not in the only possible way but by a contrast in which sin and sinlessness are alike presented in shielded light. Further natural questions such as "How serious is this condition?" lead by zigs and zags to the narrative of the passion, among others. All of this adds up to a supple and powerful mode of communication, a mixture of direct and indirect, of veiling and disclosure, offering guidance to a reader who allows the text to speak its baffling piece, yet at the same time stretching a trip wire across the path of anyone who assumes that the direct content is all that it has to offer. Whether one is inclined to call it a singular mode of communication or not, the like of it is not easy to find.

Many readers who look into the Bible for the first time

are surprised to find that parts of it, at least, and particularly the Gospels, communicate indirectly as well as directly. Little or nothing in our casual encounters with biblical passages leads us to expect that so much communication can develop, or that the texts can themselves be activated by an active reader so that personal and sometimes strenuous conversations come about. In Mark 6 the contrast between a sinless one and the rest of us dominates the scene, and once the reader clearly perceives that part of the message, a line of conversation opens up very easily. The reader of Mark 6 knows nothing about walking on water but quite a lot about drowning, sinking, and going under for the third time. A sinless one let loose in our midst! This idea is by itself jarring enough to set us wondering about familiar human incapacities that we have been trained to regard as "natural"—for instance, the fact that we can't help sinking in deep water or weakening when the food runs out or when a virus hits. Now if I put our common incapacities together with the appearance of a sinless one, it seems a lifetime would be too short to figure myself out. How can I ever expect to convince myself that it is *not* natural to drown if the boat capsizes?

An active solo reader will soon begin to notice other things, for example how closely the direct content of Mark 6 meshes with the indirect. *If* there were a condition that colored the mental as well as other dimensions of human life, what sort of contrast would offer us at least a glimpse, a seed of awareness, of its hold on us? Only a baffling contrast, it would seem, one that would freeze thought as if by novocaine. Without pretending to guess the various forms this might take—though it is easy to imagine one or two that would more than unnerve the beholder—we can say that one such contrast is given in the immediate content of Mark 6 and a number of other texts that represent a man doing the humanly impossible. On the other hand, if the texts presented no content that was (*a*) bound up with life-or-death matters and (*b*) baffling or mind-blocking, we would have no occasion or incentive to unpack a secondary content having to do with an undiscoverable condition. The humanly unrepeatable element in texts such as Mark 6 is therefore an indispensable conduit for indirect content of that sort, which cannot be put across as information on a flat trajectory, like a stock market report, but only by ricocheting off a contrast between ourselves and a sinless one. In this respect the direct and the indirect content of Mark 6 are strikingly adapted to each other.

As if it were not enough to waken a reader to a situation that human beings could not discover on their own, the verses about walking on water have at least one more jolt to deliver. The humanly impossible performance discloses, in a gentle and hintful way, the contrast between myself and the walker on the waves. Together the direct and indirect content form a complete overture capable of leading the reader into deeper conversation with the Gospel. As we noted a moment ago, the inexplicable performance functions as a sign of our humanly undiscoverable situation, revealing its grip on us by a contrast. Without the indirect sin message, the act of walking on water would be baffling but mute. The fact, however, that an indirect content, matching up with the direct, is *there to be found* is sufficient to wipe out any doubts in the reader's mind concerning whether the walk on the waves actually took place as described. To put across that particular indirect message required an unparalleled performance, one that would slide right off a graph.

It is worthwhile pausing on this point to avoid any misunderstanding. We are not engaged in proving that such and such a person walked on water, or in proving anything at all. In the mind of a solo reader who reads for personal enlightenment, stray doubts can arise over whether a specific biblical wonder really happened. These doubts are stray or out of place in that reader's mind, though they may be proper to someone doing historical research. Attending to that kind of a doubt is automatically to stop the flow of indirect content, which is the last thing this sort of reader would want to do, since it would mean backing away from the text before one had finished reading it. However, in this instance the fact that a significant indirect message lies within easy reach, and dovetails perfectly with the awesome performance, enables the reader to dismiss such doubts as annoying intruders. If the function of the wondrous performance is to deliver the indirect message, what a reversal it would be if the reader became fixated on a stray doubt of the performance!

When you reflect on how a Gospel communicates, remembering those verses from Mark 6, consider the task of composing a piece of writing that includes these features:

1. A brief narrative is placed in a larger setting, told in language simple enough to be passed on orally from one unschooled generation to the next.
2. The narrative tells of a roughly datable but scientifically incomprehensible event.
3. Under questioning, the narrative in its wider setting delivers an indirect personal message that meshes with the incomprehensible event.
4. The nature of the indirect message drives away historical doubts concerning the incomprehensible event.

This is by no means a full description of how the language of Mark 6 works, but as a partial sketch it serves our limited purpose. The task of coming up with a piece of writing that meets those four specifications is so far beyond the resources of authors I am familiar with, including a few highly resourceful ones, that the idea of someone consciously composing it strips the gears of the imagination. Perhaps, then, one could turn to hyperconscious or ecstatic authorship, but in the absence of an actual example that comes close to meeting those specifications, the suggestion lacks force. For these reasons the safest thing one can say about the mind behind the Gospels is the confession that I for one cannot make words and sentences perform so athletically. To press further, it seems to me, would be to look for the mind behind the Gospels in the sphere of speculation rather than in the Gospels themselves. As we have been observing, the Gospels, mainly in their indirect content, offer their own answers to questions about the mind behind them. What else are we glimpsing when—for example, and to begin with—we detect in them a concern to reveal an unthinkable condition, and to do it tenderly?

Again, to regard these observations as being in any sense an expression of Christian faith would wipe out the distinction between *reading* a text, or giving it, as we say, a decent hearing, and on the other hand responding by worshiping Christ as Lord. Today as in New Testament times the sin message is essentially an overture, the mere hearing of which neither presupposes that the hearer is a disciple nor turns the hearer into one.

CHAPTER FOUR

AN HOUR
WITH THE BOOK OF JONAH

To whom is the Bible addressed? Part of the answer of course is—to whole communities, to covenantal peoples: "Hear, O Israel . . ." But the Bible is also addressed to the individual human being, whether an avowed heir or heiress of its estate, someone already a believer, or a homeless stranger just looking in on the rumor that the book has something to say relative to personal needs. Each of us has an open door to the Bible and an invitation to spend some time alone with it, away from any congregation or church service.

When you read alone and read for yourself, several things are required in order to get the nourishment offered by the texts. First, as solo reader you must bring your personal needs to the reading. Whether you hunger for growth, self-understanding, peace, refreshment, or challenge, the Bible exists to meet personal hungers. For instance, a person's most basic Christian conceptions—of God, sin, faith, revelation, eternal life—can become dusty and dried out, in need of a freshening shower. Second, don't try to control what the Bible is allowed to say to you, and don't hold back your spontaneous responses and questions. When you enter, step in alone and unarmed, and be ready to reach out and pluck and taste what the Bible has to offer.

An example may make the last paragraph clearer. Turn to the book of Jonah, one of the shortest books in the Bible. A reading takes only minutes. Read through it several times, letting the text speak for itself, for often you do not know in advance which if any of your needs it may be good for. Since your purpose is to be alone with the Bible, don't look up Jonah beforehand in a biblical commentary to see how scholars classify and interpret it, though under other circumstances (in a Bible study group, for instance) scholarly questions may arise and it would be foolish not to consult the experts. At the moment, however, you have personal needs, not scholarly questions. The narrative will pretty quickly convince you that there are many things you do not share with Jonah: you have never been tapped to go out and prophesy, have never spent time in Assyria; and as for getting transported inside a fish, that is most unlikely. The entry into this little book is nevertheless quite easy, for you do have a few things in common with its main character. To begin with, you have an individual human existence, just as the narrative gives to Jonah, and you also have duties, though none so special that God has to announce them to you in person. Finally, you and Jonah share a common conception of "the God of heaven, who made the sea and the dry land" (Jonah 1:9), which is part of the Hebrew conception of God, preserved through the ages by synagogue and church as part of the biblical estate.

After this preliminary sorting out of what you share and do not share with Jonah, you may notice that in a strange way Jonah both has and does not have that ancient conception of God. He identifies himself as a Hebrew, and to that extent he has it, but in terms of his actions he makes one wonder. Jonah knows the doctrine of God—that God is above his creation, is spirit, is everywhere but invisible, is beyond our comprehension. Jonah knows the doctrine but runs afoul of it by choosing to match wits with the incomprehensible God. God lays a task on him, and Jonah puts out to sea to avoid it, as if to say, "God is after all a landlubber, so to get out of this assignment I will board a ship." A landlubber—that is easy enough to comprehend. Here, then, is something else a particular reader might share with Jonah: he had trouble lining up his day-to-day existence with the doctrine that God is unsearchable and beyond understanding, and that kind of trouble can happen to anyone. If today or tomorrow you too are required to adjust your life to that doctrine, you have the same spiritual task as Jonah. As you watch Jonah trying to make an end run around this teaching, you can almost observe the expressions on his face. His misadventures read a little like the zany sequences in a Marx Brothers film. In scenes where some unusual item is needed that no one ever carries on his person, Harpo reaches into his improbable tunic and pulls out a fish, a gourd, a snake, a duck—you name it. God keeps one step ahead of Jonah in the same way.

Despite its sometimes playful touches, the book of Jonah raises a searching personal question: "How well have I kept my own life in line with the teaching that God is beyond understanding? Has my conception of God become eroded or whittled down to the dimensions of something that the human mind can comprehend, such as the relatively superhuman power of a gale? If so, then I've got the doctrine wrong." The story of the prophet does not put this question accusingly with the force of a sledgehammer. Instead, the corrective runs gently through the text, aiming to restore the original luster to the titles of God such as "Creator" and "King of the universe." The corrective is left for Jonah to apply to himself, which he can do only by *thinking back* over his own days, just as the reader today can do. When you think back—for that is part of reading the Bible for and by yourself—what will your thoughts turn up? Perhaps a lot more, but at least this: having the same spiritual task as Jonah, the task of remembering how radically unlike us God is, you are subject to the same temporary dimming of the light, the same forgetting that came over Jonah. When that happens, you may find a use for the corrective in the prophet's story. There, gently and with a smile, God rinses the smoky film from Jonah's light.

Still on the serious side, adjusting your life to the doctrine can be uncomfortable, because in relation to God you always have to think of yourself as a little one, at least while you live on earth. This can be hard if you are a grown man or woman with little ones of your own. To be a little one means you have a blind side and can be hit from the blind side the way Jonah was hit by the unexpected storm, the unexpected gaping fish. Again, one doesn't have to reach very far to find things one has in common with Jonah.

Is the foregoing *an interpretation* of the book of Jonah? It merits no such high-sounding name. Why not simply "a reading"? The text suggests between the lines that Jonah's conception of the God of Israel relativizes the Creator's power and authority. As any rabbi could have reminded Jonah, God is not a sleepy or nearsighted monarch whose subjects can put things over on him. A mere reading can convey to anyone, but the word "interpretation" suggests special training, giftedness, and effort well beyond merely reading the text. Reading in this sense, however, does mean more than sweeping one's eyes over the surface content, which in Jonah, as in so many places in the Bible, seems to trail a parenthesis that says, "—if you get my meaning, if you get my meaning," and always with a "you," a "thou" in the clause.

In this connection, the Bible's mode of address is pitched primarily to the individual mortal, hence the importance of holding firmly to your mentality as an individual mortal if you are to read with understanding. This does not mean that you cease to belong to communities such as family, nation, and church, all of which outlast the mortal individual, but rather that you take care, in your dealings with the Scriptures, not to put on the mentality of an *immortal*. Immortals of a sort do coexist in the world with us mortals. They are more or less tightly organized institutions, managed by an unending succession of replacements. One of them is the scientific community, or call it simply science. The state is another example, and the church, or rather any denomination, is a third.

Let science be our illustration. Now if science sat down to read the Bible, that book would confront a deathless reader, one who had all the time in the world. Though the actual reading would be done by each generation of scientists, every one of whom will eventually pass away, science will not pass away, at least not before society as a whole does. Next, as any scientist will cheerfully confirm, science exists for the sole purpose of understanding phenomena. Furthermore, science is concerned only with its subject matter, and selflessly so, for it has no self to be concerned about, or to get to know, although potent and domineering egos may rise up in its ranks from time to time. Lastly, science will read the Bible in a manner very different from the way mortals like ourselves read, under very different rules and presuppositions, as we shall see shortly.

Whether science would be within its rights in reading the Bible, or whether that would amount to intercepting and peeking into other people's personal mail, is a question we must leave to scholars and lawyers. We can notice, however, how radically different we mortal individuals are from science as just described. You and I, to begin with, are not deathlessly ongoing. Next, you and I do not exist for the sole purpose of explaining phenomena or adding to the world's stock of knowledge. We also exist in and for ourselves, each person with a self to be figured out as far as his or her life permits, which means we can budget only so much time for soaking up scientific lore.

The differences between one of us and an immortal are formidable, then, and they issue in a huge further difference between two ways of reading the Bible. For instance, as regards historical matters, which make up so much of the Bible, the corporate mentality of science has made itself comfortable with a sort of postulate that states that historical events unfold in a smooth, unbroken flow of causes and effects; every event is comformable with fixed laws of nature and with rational human thought sequences. In short, only the thinkable can actually happen; stubbornly baffling events must be some kind of mistake. However, when science sits down with the Bible, it finds this postulate challenged in a variety of ways. A man does humanly impossible deeds, sees into the inscrutable future, or exhibits other kinds of knowledge not within reach of human effort. The sea parts to make a dry causeway for the Hebrews, then slams down on the pursuing Egyptians. Examples are legion. Science reads them, bites its lip, tears its hair out, and finally concludes: "These reports are not of the stuff of history. Why, everyone knows that real historical events unfold in a smooth, unbroken flow, etc." The corporate mentality of science, we are noticing, has little or no tolerance for the mysterious, the baffling, the unthinkable, the wondrous.

How different from this is the mentality of a mortal! To someone like you or me a baffling event or report can function as an overture, an attention getter, a conversation piece, a shot fired across one's bow, a sign, and above all a vehicle for conveying a secondary and personal layer of communication. But what has a corporate mentality, a professionally impersonal mentality, to do with personal messages? It filters them out. A certain baffling performance indirectly delivers a message about my sinfulness, but what should an immortal care about personal sin or the wages of it? What is the use of dropping personal hints to something that is not a person? And how does one get personal with an immortal whose paramount aim is to purge the Bible of its dark opacities and make it read like a decent work of history?

But the Bible has ways of its own, as we have noted in earlier chapters, including deceptively simple language that behaves with suppleness and power, but that can also clam up and play dead, or tonelessly repeat its surface content to readers who will not let the wondrous elements do their work—which, in many instances at least, is to initiate two-way communication with individual mortals. The reason for dwelling on this distinction between two types of mentality, individual and corporate, mortal and immortal, is that a failure to honor it can shut down basic lines of communication between the Bible and its reader. Is it possible, for example, for an individual mentality to confuse itself with the corporate one, or to identify itself with the corporate one, so that the person reads the Bible on a premise of mistaken identity? Could my individual mentality become so completely absorbed in the corporate one that I lost the power to speak in my own name? Would I then become less a person than a sort of vocal apparatus of the corporate mind? I would still be mortal in the flesh, of course, but strangely fused with an immortal that is in fact an abstraction, only a cross section of whose members exist at a given time. In a sense I would appear to gain much by becoming one with science, for I could claim in principle to understand all phenomena, but at what cost? It is by no means easy to see the deeper consequences of this—for example, whether it means that I thereby let go of myself and lose myself in the corporate mind.

Two consequences seem obvious, however. First, my

individual mentality becomes a *silent* partner in the sense that I can henceforth read in the Bible only what science can read there, and to the same extent I become a passive or an inactive reader, and an impersonal reader as well, because science cannot be expected to take personally anything that its scanner picks up. The things that my individual mentality might find in the Bible that science can't—for instance, events that would baffle me—now become off limits, along with any conduit of communication that might open up for me as a consequence of my bafflement.

The second obvious consequence is that I can never again be alone with the Bible. I may read it by myself in a locked chamber, but science with its list of no-no's and caveats and conclusions ("That cannot have happened") will be watching over my shoulder. Once I as an individual have merged my intellect with the scientific or corporate one, it is not clear how I can hold on to even a scrap of my original primitive autonomy, at least for purposes of reading the Bible.

Let us try to illustrate some of these points while the book of Jonah is fresh in our minds. It would not occur to me when reading that narrative for myself, in order to see if it contains anything I can use, to stop while Jonah marks time in the fish's belly and to ask, "How could anyone live through that?" or "Am I supposed to take this passage literally?" To depart from the plane of reading for one's own sake into a plane where one inquires into the limits of the possible is a very questionable departure, if only because humans are not in a clear position to discern those limits. Surviving three days inside a fish is a possibility in the most abstract sense of the term. Harpo Marx brought such possibilities to life when he pulled a mouse or a barstool out from under his coat. The wider category for such possibilities is the unexpected as it relates to the humorous, so a smile from the reader would be more appropriate than the question, "How is that possible?" The fact that three days inside a fish is a possibility in the weak sense does not mean that the reader of Jonah can use it for anything or that it need detain one for longer than it takes to smile. As an active reader I know what I can and cannot use, and if I keep personal needs in the penumbra of my thinking, it is unlikely that I will get hung up on a detail irrelevant to them.

When reading for yourself to see what the Bible holds for your personal needs, it is essential, then, that you go to it flying your own colors and not as an emissary of science or any other institution. It is vital also to keep lines of communication unblocked. You and I can position ourselves to catch intimations that a corporate mentality cannot catch, intimations that make sense only to a personal mentality that can internalize them. It is nonsense, for example, to say that science carries a burden of inherited sin, or that science, which has no doctrine of God's nature, has got the doctrine wrong. It makes good sense, on the other hand, to say those things of the prophet Jonah or any other individual. You or I can take them personally and check them out. Science, as a corporate mentality, cannot take anything personally.

In all our dealings with Scripture, the reader's need to keep in touch with his or her individual mentality cannot be overstressed. A biblical passage that says nothing to science, and can only be regarded by a corporate mind as a kind of scientific blunder, can speak volumes to a solo reader. In our age, to avoid confusion, it has become necessary to put into words what once went without saying, namely the differences between a personal and a corporate mentality.

CHAPTER FIVE

BEING THERE

In *The Everlasting Man*, G. K. Chesterton describes the effect of reading the Gospels "simply":

> The grinding power of the plain words of the Gospel story is like the power of mill-stones: and those who can read them simply enough will feel as if rocks had been rolled upon them.

Not everyone can read the Gospels simply enough to feel the crushing power of what Chesterton calls "the strangest story in the world." One of the things that interfere with our reading and tend to come between a reader and the text is a sort of blurry and unsettled idea of what kind of writing a Gospel is. Don't be surprised if you are not crystal clear about this. The air we breathe is so full of talk about literary forms and genres that most people haven't the time to sort it all out. The Gospels have been called, among other things, history books, works of sacred or salvation history, histories (or lives) of Jesus, biographies, memoirs, cult books, lectionaries, mixtures of history and interpretation, testimonies of post-Easter faith, passion narratives with extended introductions, existential advice clothed in mythological language, and catechetical booklets. In order to classify a document you have to position yourself far enough away from it to take in a large range of literary types and their salient characteristics, which is a far cry from moving in very close, close enough to go inside if and when it suits you.

The act of classifying a Gospel moves you away from it and away from yourself, too, into a whispering gallery of saints and scholars. On the other hand, if you move in close, you will find more personal ways of classifying it. You may end up calling it "a book that lets you inside" or "a book that rolls rocks on you," or the more traditional "good news." To whom is it that? To the needy, the down-and-out, the trapped, the hungry, the broken-hearted, the hurting, the lonely, the ignored, the no longer useful. Its overture to each one is: "You may be all those things, but you are not forgotten."

Put out of mind all you know about literary types and classifications, and then walk slowly through the seventeenth chapter of Matthew's Gospel, taking mental note of the main landmarks. What stands out to someone at ground level? First comes the transfiguration scene, and immediately after it a shrouded prediction of the passion, then the cure of a demoniac epileptic boy. Then, after a more explicit prophecy of the passion, the chapter ends with the episode about Peter paying the Temple tax. This is not exactly a seamless flow of narrative. The events don't all happen in the same corner of the nation, and no clear time sequence stands out. A reader's first impression could understandably be one of a patchy and disjointed story, somewhat like a page in a stamp album containing an assortment of commemoratives. This chapter is a good example of what led some eighteenth- and nineteenth-century biblical scholars to tear their hair out in efforts to reconstruct a Gospel, or more often all four Gospels at once, into a smooth historical treatise or a well-wrought biography.

Efforts of the research community to create new, improved or expurgated Gospels are far away from the solo reader's line of march. Reading for and by yourself, at ground level and with the naked eye, gives you an advantage, curiously enough, in discerning connections between passages that seem unrelated and are often cited separately in contexts miles apart. True, your individual mentality can take in only a little at a time, a sparrow's portion, and you might be tempted sometimes to envy the great territorial sweep of the eagle's vision, yet the sparrow can get into places closed to the eagle, and if a sparrow is what each of us basically is, this is no handicap.

As an example, read again Matt. 17:22–27. First comes the outright prediction of the Lord's suffering and death. Then, after a full stop, and in another town, the episode about the Temple tax develops. Why are these incidents placed back to back? If neither time nor place connects them, what does? What connects them is an individual mentality such as yours or mine. Peter had one, too, so you and I are in all essentials like Peter before he was invested with apostolic authority. A Gospel often presents texts that are apparently disconnected yet physically close together, the relation between them being like that of a light bulb loose in its socket. You have to give the bulb a twist; then it lights up. As a rule you do not have to call for expert help, and special apparatus would only get in the way. You step in and do the job yourself.

How? There is no formal technique to "feeling around," as one might feel around inside a refrigerator when the light bulb is not working. One way to begin is by noticing that the Temple-tax episode that ends the chapter breaks off abruptly when Jesus tells Peter to take the tax money from the mouth of the first fish he hooks. Nothing is said about Peter carrying out these instructions. Did he go down to the lake, cast out, haul in a fish, collect the money, and pay the tax? The whole impetus of the text rolls it toward that outcome. You and I are essentially like

Peter in knowing, for example, what it is like to walk down to the water, bait up, and cast a hook. This much is no challenge to the imagination. Feeling around a little more, you will remember from earlier in the chapter that Peter had recently lived through two predictions, one veiled and one outright, of his Lord's imminent suffering and death, notions that Peter could grasp, and also of his Lord's resurrection, a more mind-numbing prophecy. Who can comprehend it?

Now, as he stands waiting for a fish to nibble, Peter is living out another sort of prediction, namely that the first fish will be carrying a little something extra. Peter would see this as by far the lesser prediction, not to be compared with the personal and national calamity of losing his Lord, the long-awaited Anointed, for now all sense threatens to drain out of the messianic expectations, the ancient promises.

Meanwhile as you fish, you wait. No special permission is needed to talk this way, using a personal pronoun for example, because, for purposes of a solo reading, thou art Peter. No unusual strength of imagination is required, either, since all the components of your reflection are given in the printed text, and it is all something like feeling around and tightening a bulb.

As you wait with the slack line in your hand, with the words of the other prediction, the repeated one, the calamitous one, still echoing, the prospect of that sudden tautening of the line as a fish strikes takes on a terrible significance. Two tax payments out of the whole population would not amount to a life-or-death matter, but if the instructions about the fish check out, if the lesser and wildly improbable prediction comes true, then all hope must vanish for softening the greater prophecy of suffering and death. You hold the line and wait, hoping nothing will bite, hoping it's too hot or the fish are nesting or the bait has floated loose from the hook. This time there will be no glad start at a tug on the line. Your heart will begin to sink and will hit bottom at the first sign of a silvery glint in the fish's mouth as you haul it in. And your steps to the tax collector's booth with the cold, hard coin in your hand will be slow, heavy, joyless. What could give sweeter relief than to go back and tell your Lord you fished until dark, and after dark, and nothing took the bait? Then comes a quick pull on the line.

You feel around, then give the bulb a twist, and the connection is made. Where does the light go on? Not on the page, but in the reader's individual mentality. Can we say that the narrative of the Temple-tax money is *about* the prophecy of suffering and death? Not exactly, or not directly at any rate. But the two prophecies would connect mercilessly in Peter's mind, the lesser reinforcing the greater. When joined together in the medium of an individual's mind, the odd scrap of foreknowledge concerning the fish dovetails with the unbearable foretelling of the worst thing of all. But the bulb must be made to touch the base of the socket. For this to happen, you need no special learning, but you do need to remember and use what you have in common with Peter, an individual mentality that can appreciate, among other things, the "great sadness" that sat with him as he waited for that unlikely fish to bite.

Would Peter have been nonplussed by his Lord's uncanny knowledge of goings-on under the surface of that lake? It seems very doubtful that he would give much thought to that while the dark shape of personal and national tragedy loomed up ahead. The strangeness of it would never wear off, but Peter would have no more idea of how to penetrate it than you or I. Let rabbis explain such things, not fishermen. And except for its fitting with such precision into the greater and darker prophecy, this incident might after a time have faded from his mind.

Afterward, on his way to pay the tax, would Peter perhaps ask himself, "How is such knowledge possible?" But why bother guessing? You are Peter. How would you have reacted? Here is one possibility:

"I will do as I was told and pay the tax, but what sense does even the Temple make any more? The sense of everything is in collapse. What baffles me is that he knows where the money is, but lets it gather dust. He has the hand of power as well, but chooses not to make it into a fist. Nothing could stand in his way. He could command an army if we still had an army, then make himself king once we had a nation to ourselves again. But a messiah who lives in a lean-to and spends his time with a dozen mostly raggedy and unperfumed types like myself from around the docks, when he knows the inner workings of the imperial councils! It makes no sense to me.

"And now this thing today dissolves away the last hope that he could be wrong about what's in store. If he goes under, doesn't his whole kingdom go with him? That part about rising on the third day loses me, as he must have realized when he said it. Three days in the grave is about as dead as can be. And there up ahead is the tax collector, looking surprised at the sight of me. I hope he has the bad manners to ask how I came by this lump sum. If he does, I will uncork another surprise for him by telling the truth."

There is of course no reason to suppose that these were exactly Peter's thoughts, or that they even come close. They are presented only as an example of how an individual mentality might react to those events. To react instead by asking, "How could he possibly have known about that fish?" would be to raise what is obviously a question for a research team that might carry on through generations of replacements without reaching a firm verdict. For someone in Peter's circumstances to be dwelling on such a question would mean that he had slipped into distraction or forsaken all personal and human priorities.

Commentators have explored legal, moral, political, and theological wrinkles of the Temple-tax narrative, and rightly so, for the text sounds all those vibrations in addition to the chord of disaster it struck for Peter as he lived through the lesser prophecy. One recent authority, J. D. M. Derrett, in his *Law in the New Testament*, has even established, through team research on coins and fishes, that the coin must have been a Tyrian shekel and the fish could only have been a *Clarius lazera* of the catfish family. Earnest and careful detective work goes into such findings, work that no solitary researcher could hope to advance very far. A scholar undertaking research of this sort has to maintain contact with a far-flung web of colleagues, with those who know most about the coins and fishes of Palestine during Roman times. Research in any form, and however creditable it may be, stands in bold contrast to someone's spending time alone with that Gospel text.

Taken by itself, the episode of the Temple tax is one of those New Testament events which tempt many scholars to apply the term "legend" whenever the collegial mentality has trouble digesting an unrepeatable event or performance. As a result, much of what the Gospel communicates indirectly does not register on the corporate intelligence. This shows the importance of keeping in constant touch with your individual intelligence in order to catch the indirect content along with the direct. Your original equipment is not bound by a rule observed in certain schools of biblical research, namely that each little section of text must be understandable all by itself, like each paragraph in a well-written history textbook, which consists entirely of direct communication. That is not the only mode of effective communication, and it is certainly not the only mode we find in the Bible. Whether you are a believer or not (for faith is not required in order to read with understanding), if you want to know what is in the Bible,

what it contains for you, you would do well not to sur-
render your personal intellect to the control of any corporate one to the extent of adopting its ways of speaking and
its reading techniques.

If you look back for a moment at your reading of Matthew 17, you can notice a couple of things about the style
in which a Gospel is written. Many of the incidents are
loosely sequenced and lacking in obvious connective tis-
sue such as we should expect to find in any well-wrought
novel or movie script. Since a Gospel brings "good news,"
one might think of comparing it with a newsreel or, better, with a series of film clips reviewing the life of a presi-
dent or royal personage, with infancy pictures, highlights
of the person's career, and finally the funeral procession.
Yet there is an important sense in which a Gospel is not
filmable at all, though not because the task would put any
great strain on special effects experts. A movie is its
director's baby, and you and I as viewers have to sit pas-
sively in a darkened theater with no control over what appears on the screen. For example, film editors could put
together footage in which the actor playing Peter casts a
line into the lake and shortly thereafter pulls in a flopping
fish. With no apparent break in the photography you
would see him pry the coin out of the fish's mouth, toss
the fish back, and set out toward the tax collector's sta-
tion. That is part of the direct content of the Temple-tax
episode, though it is only implied in the written Gospel.

However, you could not stop the film and step inside
that scene yourself. You could not take part in Peter's
waiting for the first tug, because the director knows his art
and has set the film's pace in keeping with the rule: "No
unnecessary stopping and waiting." As the scene shifts
quickly to the tax collector's office, you will have no time
to live out the lesser prophecy under the shadow of the
greater and grimmer one, no time even to make the connection. And the scene itself will afterward seem no more

than a senseless stunt, a bit of biblical mumbo jumbo in
another medium. The sense, the dreadful sense of the incident will have passed you by. In short, the movie may
deliver to you the direct content of Matthew's text, but
there is no way it can deliver the indirect. To take in the
indirect content your personal mentality has to make itself contemporary with the event, and it requires time to
do this. You have to be there, and being there is precisely
what the written Gospel makes possible for a solitary, active reader.

Though a Gospel's style of writing bears a superficial resemblance to a number of different literary genres, as we
noted at the start of this chapter, it is not easy to find a
class of written works combining direct and indirect communication in the manner of a Gospel, or exhibiting the
"loose bulb in socket" kind of connection we observed between the two closing passages in Matthew 17. Is there a
standard literary form in which an apparently dead bulb
in an apparently juiceless socket lights up when given a
twist? Do we know of other writings about past events
that allow the individual of a much later time to become
contemporary with those events, not by flexing the imagination but by sharing effectively in the events so as to be
able to spot connections that would otherwise escape notice? We will not pretend to settle questions like these,
whose answers depend on a survey of world literature
and on special scholarly training. The closest familiar
genre that comes to mind is the private person-to-person
communication, written or vocal.

If there is ever a scholarly consensus on the wider genre
that a Gospel belongs to, one could still ask whether that
consensus would shed any light on the aspects of a Gospel that stand out most vividly to the nonspecialized but
active solo reader. For as you move into Gospel material
at ground level, gloveless against thistles and with no
dark glasses to protect your eyes from glare, almost every

section of every chapter reports some kind of local disturbance. Some of the turbulence occurs only at the level of language (utterances with unexpected, baffling, or offensive combinations of words), some of it shows agitation in official circles both Jewish and Roman, some erupts in rural settings, some in the sea, the sky, or other natural environs, and some even in sealed tombs. In the Temple-tax incident the turbulence occurs in the mind and heart of Peter and is not related directly in the text, but only when an individual reader links that text to the preceding one. Someone fishing a few yards away from Peter might have noticed nothing at all.

CHAPTER SIX

ALONE WITH LUKE

It is becoming harder and harder for an educated man or woman to be alone with the Bible, particularly someone who is exposed to modern research *about* the Bible, if only through book review sections in newspapers. The techniques of historical research tend in the opposite direction from reading on your own, for research means team reading, team analysis, team interpretation, and it is difficult to imagine how things could be otherwise when you consider the vast lode of material. The teamwork stretches back over centuries and shows no signs of running out of steam or fresh personnel.

The other side of the coin is also important and can be expressed just as briefly. The Scriptures are not addressed to a historical research team but primarily to human individuals and specific covenantal communities whose ways of thinking have been shaped largely by the Scriptures themselves, not by an extraneous tradition and certainly not by the norms and requirements of historical research, which go back only a couple of centuries. This situation creates the possibility of static or interference between the team's way of reading the Bible and the individual's way or the covenantal community's way, for the reading techniques are radically distinct. They split approximately along the dividing line between personal and impersonal.

The Gospel of Luke, for example, aims at involving the reader personally, and the plain reader aims at drawing personal nourishment from Luke, whereas the researcher, bent on the team's purpose of extracting hard information about the past, has to keep personal concerns out of the way, for they would be foreign bodies in a finished piece of historical research. Said another way, the researcher, in a professional capacity, tunes in to what Luke communicates directly and seeks to establish its authenticity by applying the team's criteria. Reading is a very different matter for the individual with his or her own life, death, and other personal concerns in mind. This reader tunes in to the direct communication but understands from past experience or the rumor of nourishment that the immediate content often serves as a vehicle for that which is not, and sometimes cannot be, presented directly, and that reading it in a personal way means allowing the immediate material to deliver its indirect and personal payload. If it delivers on that wavelength, and keeps delivering, then it meets the *individual's* criterion for authenticity.

It may take hard conscious effort to isolate yourself with the first two chapters of Luke, even under ideal physical circumstances, for you will recall remarks, many of them skeptical, that flow from team reading about those extraordinary happenings in the lives of Zechariah, Elizabeth, Mary, and Joseph. Can you put those remarks out of mind and read those pages as if for the first time? If you can, then the texts will be able to function. The baffling ones will stay baffling, and there are plenty of those, including a text about one unborn infant recognizing another. As you read the two chapters, you will understand some things immediately—why, for example, those four people in particular found themselves disbelieving, troubled, frightened, perplexed. The thing you have in common with those people, the human life you are living out day by day, simply cannot take certain kinds of intrusion in stride. They are too upsetting.

As we noted earlier, reports of local turbulence form the main tissues, the flesh and bone of a Gospel when a single reader reads it, and the opening chapters of Luke confirm that judgment. The turbulence here is mostly in private lives associated with the unborn infants, and it barely foreshadows the public and cyclonic disturbances in later chapters. The humbler turbulence is for the sake of what is getting ready to happen, as the angel's remarks to Mary and the prophecies in the Temple repeatedly declare. Fingers keep pointing to what is up ahead, and the conventional response of the human eye is to look where the fingers point, but here we can make an exception and stop to notice some things. A Gospel does not ask you to imagine anything—in fact its central message defies imagination—but it does ask you to become a noticer, and to that end it lays out for you what it thinks is worth noticing. It does not ask you to believe each report of turbulence as you read it or as part of your reading it, for that is a researcher's style of believing, one chip at a time as he works on the historical mosaic. You are not into believing, but rather giving Luke a decent human reading.

You will not notice everything worth noticing on one walk through those chapters, but something you might notice is a strange atmosphere. Notice, then react. For example, any reader might begin: "We all know these chapters lead up to the story of Christ, but what a strange way to prepare for the main event! Angels come by (whatever angels are); an older woman and a young virgin find themselves pregnant, the virgin under ambiguous circumstances; and the older woman's husband is struck dumb but recovers. These obscure events pave the way for the crowning moment of this people's history, the coming of the Messiah/Redeemer. I have to admit that the words 'Behold, I am the handmaid of the Lord,' coming from a girl just over the threshold of womanhood, and when her consent spelled all kinds of trouble ahead, are so full of trust that a cagey type like myself can scarcely begin to comprehend them. But what about the rest of it, the obscure people and an archangel who is not too good at convincing Zechariah? Where is the majesty? Where is the majesty in a virginal conception that leaves room for poor taste and local small talk to joke around with low-down variations on that theme? Surely if the God of Israel decided to intervene decisively in human affairs, there would be cleaner-cut ways of doing it."

If someone reacted to Luke 1–2 in this way, speaking personally and not as the representative of a professional community of philosophers, scholars, or literary critics, the reaction would be entirely in order. The Gospel has made its overture, this individual has made an initial response, and now conversation has begun. Persistence will correct any misunderstandings in the reaction, and meanwhile the person has raised several important questions: Why the obscure setting and characters? Why such potential for scandalizing people? Why the tightly restrained show of power?

If the individual closes the book and stands pat on that initial reaction, the Gospel will slip back into its mute disguise as an ancient document. However, as we noted earlier, a Gospel has its own ways of replying to questions that originate in a solo reader's own mentality. If he or she is serious enough to put those questions to the Gospel, searching the texts for leads, asking for help when stuck, trying cowpaths in the Psalms or Wisdom or the epistles to see where they come out, and always keeping the mind open to surprises, the conversation can develop into something lively and revealing.

There are texts, for example, that speak of obscurity and lowliness, texts that speak to the obscure and lowly person, and texts that speak to the advantaged ones who ignore that person. There are texts that hint or warn about scandal, others in which someone cries out scandalized, and still others in which someone puts herself under threat of scandal. In one text God is praised for restraining his power, while in another place someone howls at God to unleash that power killingly. There are texts in which God's hiddenness is acclaimed, and others where someone begs God to come out swinging at this or that enemy. The margins in many editions of the Gospels are studded with references to analogous passages in both Testaments, sometimes so numerous that it would drive a reader crazy to check out all of them. However, to someone whose questions are specific, for instance about God's fondness for obscurity, scandal, and restraint, those references can help.

Another thing you might have noticed in glancing back over Luke 1–2 is a difference between the angel's approaches to Zechariah and to Mary. To Zechariah, Gabriel came with the promise of an answer to prayer. Elizabeth would bear him a longed-for son, and moreover a son destined for a mighty mission in the tradition of Elijah. There was no question of asking Zechariah's consent to a development he had been praying for. To Mary, though, the angel came to ask her permission. God was asking her permission, through Gabriel, to confer on her a role she could not fathom and had certainly never prayed would be hers. Her reply was in the form of consent, unconditional permission, though of course she did not know what she was letting herself in for beyond the promise that she would conceive, bear, and name a male child. It is the element of God's asking permission to do something to one of his creatures that makes the scene between Mary and the angel a cameo of the kind of faith relationship that was to become an earmark of Christianity after the new church came into being. Christ, too, would ask the individual's permission.

This point may help clarify a suggestion made earlier, namely that for a human being to read the Bible with understanding, and to discern what it proposes for one personally, does not require faith. Christian faith, as the term applies to an individual, includes giving unconditional consent to Christ to put the person through whatever is necessary to "save" that person or bring that person into the "Kingdom," including a complete factory overhaul if needed, and then sticking by that permission trustingly, no matter what happens. However, making out a blank check to someone you can't even get a good look at—and paying up cheerfully whenever he floats a due bill into your life—sounds close to being the hardest thing of all and something we should keep quite distinct in our minds from just getting to know the Bible. In short, it is a bad analogy to think of Scripture as a locked estate and faith as the key that would magically let me inside—if only I had it! The gate is not padlocked, but the latch is positioned for people on foot, in wheelchairs, and the like. Anyone on a high horse has to dismount.

As part of paying attention to yourself along with the texts, ask yourself whether Luke 1–2 gave you any headaches with regard to *believing* items in the narrative, such as angelic visits, the virginal conception, an unborn infant jumping for joy, or Zechariah's muteness and sudden cure, all of which stand far enough outside the usual run of events to resist quick and easy understanding. They have their stubbornly baffling side; the characters in the narrative acknowledge that. If you were able to read through the two chapters without those particulars slowing you down, that is all to the good, for the elements of the narrative do not present themselves like so many puppies in a pet shop window, wagging and whining for attention. If there are any problems connected with *believ-*

ing what we find in the first two chapters of Luke—and it is by no means obvious that there are—an individual reader can at any rate suspend all matters of believing until after giving the text a personal perusal. If a certain wing of scholarship has a rule stating that each bit of text must be understood before it can be said to be read, this will not bother a solo reader in the least. As a human being, this reader can tolerate a certain level of uncomprehended material, for example the intrusions of an angel telling of important things to come. Does the individual need to have some firm data about angels in order to understand a sentence like "Some unparalleled things are getting ready to happen"? No, the individual understands that the accent is on what is up ahead, and can look in that direction, aware that the angel (whatever it may be) is calling attention not to itself but to something yet to come. And if a renowned man of learning has just created a buzz among his colleagues by asking how it is possible for a bodiless angelic visitor to make vocal sounds, this will not alarm the reader who has understood the sentence and is looking on ahead. If someone famous is afflicted with a charley horse, should you and I limp?

Local disturbances, intrusions, break-ins—many of the incidents in Luke 1–2 have that character, with rumors of less localized turbulence still to come. It is interesting that millions of us flock to special effects films about UFOs, amiable little pet-like extraterrestrials, endearing robots, and misty but friendly shapes in the doorways of spacecraft. Why do they come to visit earth from other solar systems, those friendly ones? (The marauding types, who want to steal our oxygen or raid our blood banks, we can leave out of this account.) The answer is usually vague. Sometimes they want to warn our scientists or politicians or the superpowers against messing around with plague germs or genes or plutonium. The visitors, as often represented, are of higher intelligence than ourselves, as shown by their terrific technology—and culturally ahead of us as well, as shown by the loud music. In characters like Superman, they exercise more-than-human powers against forces such as organized crime.

As we sit in the dark, sheltered theater, surrounded by gasps, chuckles, and loud music, scary moments may occur as well, but these fleeting excitements come under the heading "thrills." In this entertainment medium the price of admission buys us the assurance that we can forget ourselves for a couple of hours; the great fuss on the screen, the assault on our eyes and ears, is not about us but about those characters on the screen. There is nothing personal.

Luke's chapters, too, deal with intrusions into our human, earthly sphere, but intrusions of a very different kind. The texts are set up to "involve" you, though not, as in the film about intruders from space, to whirl you away in artful distraction and make you so "involved" in the action that you forget yourself. In Luke the idea is to do away with all distraction, loud music, and special effects, so that you can remember yourself and become involved precisely by remembering yourself, the person you wake up to every morning.

Why *these* intrusions into the human sphere? As promised privately by an angel, a hill-country woman conceives beyond her childbearing years, and then her cousin, a young maiden, also conceives, but with no male seed; one infant is to become a harbinger of redemption, the other its bearer. Viewed from certain altitudes, the prophecies of Simeon in the Temple about the child of Mary sound very much like the outlines of a great plan set in motion by a power higher than humanity and programmed to run its course no matter what individual humans think or do. From those altitudes the plan of salvation is a little like decisions taken in the top-floor board room to maneuver a corporation through a financial crisis, while the employees down to the humblest levels go

about their jobs mostly unaware of what is happening as
they assemble products, ship and receive goods, sweep
floors, and clean up in the cafeteria. Top management is
behind the scenes calling the shots that will shape the
fates of all these human lives.

Yet to a personal intelligence reading Luke close up, it
is not at all like that, and the first sign that things are
otherwise appears when God, through the angel, promises Zechariah and Elizabeth a son and then asks Mary's
permission to plant the seed of a son in her. Suppose we
ask again: Why *these* intrusions? In earthly terms, in understandable terms, what is supposed to come about in
consequence of these two infants getting born? The sharp-
est words come from Simeon, who tells Mary that a sword
will pierce her soul, and that the thoughts of many hearts
will be revealed (Luke 2:35). In another translation, the *secret* thoughts of many will be revealed. These are hints,
whispers of the effects of these births on ordinary people
like you and me, and not just in Israel, for the Gentiles
have already been mentioned (Luke 2:32). To someone lis-
tening in on these prophecies at ground level, or in the
shadows of the Temple, or alone with Luke's texts a thousand years later, this will be a strange thought. All these
portentous events, it seems, are aimed at turning inside
out the secret thoughts of people like you and me. Here
an individual might reflect: "I daresay any person may
harbor some secret thoughts, including myself, and perhaps so secret that I would not care to talk them over even
with myself, but I would hardly think this fact worth making a major fuss over. But according to this prophecy,
those thoughts are what the Gospel turbulence is all
about, as if those were the most important thing about me!
If that is what all the commotion is about—the local turbulence in the opening chapters and the stormier stuff
later on—then I must admit it deals with exceedingly personal matters, but I am deeply puzzled as to why the God

of Israel, in his incomprehensible majesty, should take an intimate interest in such things!"

It is puzzling, but to an individual reader a puzzle can become an occasion for expressing puzzlement and throwing it right back at the Gospel: "Why do you open up this business about my secret thoughts when clearly, in my own mind, the most important thing about me is how much I've cheerfully paid out to raise my family right?" (or however someone might fill in this blank). As a solitary reader, you will find a real spur to conversation with the Gospel whenever you find yourself in head-on disagreement with it, particularly on a question as personal as: What is the most important thing about me?

When you are reading Luke 1–2 by and for yourself, the virginal conception of Jesus will not present itself as a stumbling block to belief. In the first place, the question of believing that it happened is quite independent of reading those chapters to see for yourself what they contain and whether they link up at any point with your own existence. Secondly, the virginal conception is not the type of incident that calls for a response all by itself. Reading it alone, you will immediately perceive that the extraordinary conception is a form of advance notice—at first to an audience of only one—that the child thus conceived will be no ordinary child. The same reader will realize right away that the virginal conception cannot provide credentials for that child; the mode of his conception can become significant only in retrospect, in the light of what the child goes on to become or to do. A virgin's conceiving a child is too improbable and unpublic an event to guarantee that such and such further events will follow. Just the reverse is true; later events can draw the lion's share of the solo reader's attention, leaving the texts about a virginal conception firmly in place but now overshadowed by what has since come to pass.

Luke's first two chapters, you will notice, list the events

in chronological order—conception, birth, maturation—but this is not necessarily the order in which a natural reader will seize them or be seized by them. For these are private happenings that might well have come to light only *after* the climactic events of later chapters had come and gone. The fact that Luke put them first in his written Gospel does not mean they will not function as an *appendix* or *postscript* to the rest of the Gospel in the natural reader's ranking of things. In the form of an appendix, the first two chapters might say in effect, "Incidentally, John the Baptist was conceived out of due time, etc.; and incidentally, Mary gave God permission, etc." This shows how wand-like and supple the concept of "literary form" is, and also how deceiving and procrustean it can be to absorb the Gospels into any larger genus of writings.

For reasons like these one can argue that texts affirming the virginal conception of Jesus will not create snags for an individual mentality as it searches out what it can use. Still, it is well to remember that God's leaving a chosen young woman with child is not something that your thinking apparatus or mine can render transparent, for it includes the cryptic factor "God" (or the cryptic factor "nothing will be impossible," as in Luke 1:37).

CHAPTER SEVEN

THE ACCENT
OF THE ETERNAL

For quite some time the notion has been circulating that the Scriptures come down to us saturated with ancient culture, in Hebrew, Greek, Egyptian, Sumerian, and other assorted flavors. Human language, that culture-stained and time-conditioned inheritance of ours, is after all the Bible's medium of communication, and even if God himself adopts that medium, he confines himself within its cultural horizons and the limits of its expressive power. As a result, the so-called Word of God speaks at every point with a human and historical accent. In short, no matter what page you open to, there is no pure, clear accent of the eternal to be found in the Bible.

This notion has a safe-sounding ring, but how carefully reasoned is it? Above all, how do those who repeat this notion *read* the Scriptures? As we have seen, there are various techniques for reading, for example with personal needs in mind or out of mind, and by yourself or as a member of a research team, and with the naked eye or aided by the latest finely ground optical systems. If you look at the Bible *as* a cultural deposit, and thus tune your expectations to pick up echoes of the customs, idioms, and characteristic thought patterns of earlier societies, the Bible will not disappoint you. Its pages are rife with such echoes. But that is precisely the trouble with preclassifying biblical material, even under as broad and vaporous a heading as "cultural phenomena." If in fact the accent of the eternal has been preserved between those covers, it will not appear as a cultural difference, since the eternal is the acultural; and it may not appear at all to a mind attuned to cultural differences such as nuances of temple architecture.

Despite the safe sound, it makes very little sense to conclude that the Bible contains no clear accent of the eternal unless one starts out with a fairly well-formed idea of what such an accent would be like. Then a search might indeed prove negative. However, in the absence of a well-formed idea, there is no genuine search either, and therefore only a make-believe negative result.

What would the voice of the timeless, the eternal, sound like? What would it be like for that voice to hold forth in *language?* This is the kind of question we need to press in order to shake off the spell cast by the notion that everything linguistic is culture-conditioned and everything culture-conditioned is all-too-human and of human devising from start to finish.

What we should be looking for in the Bible, it seems, are trackless ideas, unthinkable thoughts, foreign bodies, mind stoppers. However, before you take up this challenge and begin your search for the unthinkable, pause long enough to make sure you are on your own and reading for yourself. Make sure, in other words, that you are alone, that no one is monitoring your reading, that no distinguished and immortal brotherhood or corporate understanding oversees your task. As you look for signatures of the eternal in those pages, remember that they exist only for mortals.

If you read as a mortal, the signatures will be plain enough. You have already seen some in our earlier discussions, for example in the light that plays between the layers of Genesis 1–2, and in the way the language of miracle works. This time turn to the epistle to the Philippians, where Paul is speaking of Christ:

> Though he was in the form of God, [he] did not count equality with God a thing to be grasped, but emptied himself, taking the form of a servant, being born in the likeness of men. (Phil. 2:6–7)

There is more to the passage, but let us stop here. In a section on humility Paul is invoking the memory of a flesh-and-blood individual who for some years was his contemporary and fellow countryman, whether their paths ever crossed or not. This former contemporary was originally divine, says the apostle. Paul is fully in possession of the Hebrew doctrine of God, and he knows better than most how taboo it is to identify the Holy One with anything or anyone on earth. A Greek god or goddess might take on human form, and so might one of the Hindu deities, but for Israel's God such an idea was strictly off limits. God is not one of the gods. Yet Paul makes the forbidden connection, and makes it in a hymnlike tone of awestruck praise. He makes it as a believer, a man of faith, but you and I do not need an iota of faith merely to read those verses and ask, "Whose idea is expressed there?"

Whose idea is it? If there is an idea floating around, surely it is somebody's. Ideas do not grow on trees or condense on the grass like morning dew. Thoughts or ideas occur to human beings, language users, who frequently write them down and keep track of them. Well, then, perhaps this is Paul's idea, except that Paul is at some pains to deny it. In other places Paul has some ideas of his own, and identifies them as his, but this is not one of them. He denies, in fact, that any human could so much as conceive of this idea (I Cor. 2:7–9). And his denial makes a kind of immediate sense, for the Most High emptying himself of glory to enter into earthly servitude is not the sort of happening that humans are equipped to perceive and then tell others about. Nobody, that is, would have occasion to say to a companion, "Don't look now, but that fellow behind you, the one pouring wine at the next table, was originally equal to God but decided to throw in his lot with us." Do we know of any parallel, any precedent for bringing forth that idea? Paul sets it in his epistle like an inlay, acknowledging with burning gratitude that the event happened; but where would he get such an idea? He reminds the Christians of Philippi that God spent some time on earth in a disguise that no one could penetrate, and the harder we stare at that idea, the glassier our eyes become. Isn't it practically the same as saying there is nothing new to report?

It would be very strange if someone tried to argue that Paul extracted that idea from his culture or from the Greco-Roman culture that coexisted with his. It would amount to blasphemy and a grammatical outrage in his own culture, and the Greco-Roman lacked an essential element, the Hebrew conception of God. But we need make no farfetched guesses about where Paul got that idea. He got it from the same source you and I have access to, namely one or more Gospel accounts, whether written or sealed in the memory of the early church and passed along by word of mouth. There and there alone (apart from veiled prophecies) do we find news of the happening that Paul's verses celebrate. Those intimations are not given in the same words Paul uses but in the turbulent episodes, visible and palpable, touched off by the one who, in Paul's words, emptied himself. Paul gives us in abbreviated form what the Gospels spell out detail by detail.

Sometime when you are alone with those verses, ask yourself whether you are looking at a human thought in what they say. Allow yourself plenty of time to make up your mind on this question, for it will not be easy to persuade yourself that there is a thought loose in the world without a human mental apparatus behind it. And even if you come to that conclusion, nothing sensational will follow from it directly, though it may produce some quiet aftereffects. For one thing, you will become very wary of the notion that the eternal has no accent of its own, or that every verse in the Bible is greasy with human culture. "Culture," unfortunately, is one of those catchall terms that wagging tongues find irresistible. To catch the accent of the eternal, on the other hand, the first requirement is to let the eternal do its proper share of the talking. You will be suspicious, too, of the claim that God's powers of communication are in any way curtailed by the human medium of language. If Paul's verses are on target, God let loose in our midst the rumor of his boundless caring and daring.

With that brief reading from Philippians behind us, we are in a better position to notice a few dry and not very important matters, as follows:

Item: A sea of ink has been dipped dry by people trying to separate what is historical in the New Testament from what is not. If you are a solo reader, such concerns form no part of your personal task, nor need they threaten you as something down the road that will sooner or later demand payment in full. Paul has moored his epistle to historical bedrock, and with the strictest economy of means. Referring to Jesus he says, "*His* state was divine, etc."— and in this "his" the historical, or as much of it as the solo reader will ever require, sits firmly on the calendar of the centuries. For the subject of "his" is not only Paul's one-time contemporary but is, or was, exceptionally well known to the authorities and even boasted, as police jargon expresses it, a record of priors.

If on the other hand Paul had left us a sentence like this:

"A preexistent divine being emptied itself of majesty and appeared on earth as a man," then the borderline between history and nonhistory would immediately take on a blurry look, and it would be well worth the solo reader's time to try to connect that strange event with some definite man.

Item: The epistle to the Philippians contains this striking figuration: he emptied himself of majesty. The majesty is unthinkable; human thought, in other words, does not know where to round itself off on this matter and place the closing period. The idea of the God of Israel divesting himself of majesty throws human thought back on itself and sets it to thinking furiously, thinking about how the thinker could possibly relate to this past happening other than by figuring it out, which is out of the question.

The solo reader will have no trouble perceiving that those verses of Paul are not description or eyewitness testimony but praise and thanksgiving, and that Paul is stepping forward as someone for Christians to imitate, someone praising and at the same time giving instruction in how to praise. My words, he is saying, are a good way to praise.

Item: Most of the time when reading for yourself you will not need to *interpret* biblical texts, and so it is with those verses of Paul. The tone of praise, gratitude, and worship is interpretation enough. When an expression stumps you, the task of getting clearer is usually rather minor. You look up a puzzling phrase such as "poor in spirit" or, better still, ask someone. Speaking generally, there is no need to master an author's complete works in order to find your footing in them.

Item: The natural reader will have a sense of what he or she is lacking. For example, having noticed those verses of Paul in Philippians, a non-Christian reader coming new to this material might remark: "The idea of God forsaking glory in favor of human slavery has more than enough punch, but what purpose does it serve? I am not helped by reading further that the slave accepted death on a cross, since Paul cites no obvious purpose for that, either. So in order for those verses to say anything revealing to me, there must be something more, and I don't mean the resurrection, which is another stunner. Obviously Paul means to be pointing back to a bygone actuality, but that is just what I'm saying is not enough. It has to be the kind of actuality I can bring myself up against."

Someone who responds in this way is expressing a very real gap in understanding what the New Testament is all about, though it is a remediable gap. The authors of epistles can point back to the man Jesus and preach him, they can worship and glorify him, but they cannot present him. He presents himself—in the Gospels. Epistles are genuinely ancient documents, letters to the then-young churches, to individuals, or to Christians generally. You can learn much from them, but understanding their dynamics presupposes that you have been exposed to Gospel material, which is textured in ways that allow you to step inside on the strength of what you have in common with the persons Jesus healed as well as those he offended. The epistles, in contrast, are quite straightforward instruction, some of it as difficult as anything in the Bible. But the epistles do not have the further aspect of a disguised meeting place.

CHAPTER EIGHT

INSPIRATION

Someone who is just striking up a personal acquaintance with the Scriptures will do well to keep away from the specialized vocabularies of professional theology and Scripture scholarship. Reading purposefully for yourself requires no heavy equipment. In these chapters we have also stayed away from direct questions about the inspiration (and hence the authority) behind the biblical works. Our purpose has not been to dodge hard questions so much as to describe and illustrate a style of reading that allows the Bible to answer those questions out of its own resources and to answer them obliquely or "by the way," yet to the individual's satisfaction.

A church or denomination will affirm the divine inspiration of the Old and New Testaments as an expression of its own authority and its faith in its mandate to serve God in a Christian spirit. If you are an active church member, by reading the Bible on your own you can come to appreciate more fully its power to inspire large assemblies of worshipers from one generation to the next. For many an individual alone with the Scriptures, however, membership in a church may be an option somewhere off in the future. Yet for such a reader, too, the Bible has ways of letting on that it is not just another book in our civilization's glut of books. Most Gospel material, for example, consists of language shaped into chambers or hollows so that you can step inside and place yourself actively on the scene. Insofar as the Gospels' divine inspiration reveals itself to an individual, it does so indirectly through the power to let you in and to get personal with you, assuming you permit that to happen.

What could be more personal than for someone to reveal me to myself, to show me that I am held fast in an inexplicable bondage? Could I have revealed this to myself? As we noted in our discussion of Mark 6, some surprising effects of sin get revealed in a contrast between ourselves and a sinless one. In revealing each disciple to himself or herself in that strange and baffling light, the revealer exhibits his authority. And now, centuries later, by letting me inside to undergo the same sobering experience, the Gospel text shows that the authority of the revealer is not something that was there in those days and is gone today, but something enduring, undying. This is what is meant by calling a piece of writing inspired: one is saying that the authority behind it is still fresh and in working order.

All of this arises from a mere *reading* experience, remember, basically a pre-Christian kind of experience, with faith perhaps a later event. Here someone might remark that reading a Gospel in this way has brought people to their knees and led them on the path to faith. But can it not also repel people and turn them away muttering that they want nothing to do with such a challenge? Both kinds of reaction are amply recorded in the New Testament.

To approach the idea of divine inspiration from another angle, read once more the Prologue to the Fourth Gospel (John 1:1–18). The powerful opening lines sound echoes of Genesis:

In the beginning was the Word, and the Word
was with God, and the Word was God.

A buildup follows like a mighty wave forming:

The true light that enlightens every man was
coming into the world.

It crests in the lines:

The Word became flesh and dwelt among us,
full of grace and truth; we have beheld his
glory.

In earlier times the Prologue's language convinced readers as acute as Augustine and Chrysostom that it is beyond the power of human beings to speak as John speaks,
and their conviction offers a kind of testimony that the
Gospel author was divinely inspired. This testimony is
personal, however, and imbued with faith, and there is no
reason why a reader of today, looking into the Bible for
the first time, should leap to the same conclusion.

The Prologue stands like a granite pillar inscribed with
the words, "The greatest event of all happened here." If
you ask. "*What* happened here?" the inscription does not
tell you. The Word was made flesh, it says, but what was
that like? The Prologue doesn't go into much detail. It is a
retrospect on an event which, for all it tells us, might have
taken place quietly, stirring up no turbulence at all. The
Prologue speaks only in the vaguest terms about Jesus,
giving no hint of anything he said or did and little of how
his life began or ended; it proclaims an incomprehensible
event but gives us no idea of what someone's coming in
contact with it was like. You can read the Prologue fifty
times and still be left with the question: "But what does it
say actually took place on that site? What was it like to
have been there at the time?" Knock and tap as you will
on the stone pillar, you will get no answer to your human
question from the Prologue. It confronts you with the ver-

bal silhouette of a once-only event. You can walk around it and stand in its shadow, but you cannot go inside. The Prologue is Christianity in outline, at the highest level of abstraction. It is Christianity in the act of standing us off, defying us to comprehend it. It is Christianity cutting us off from itself, yet this can hardly be the intention of the Gospel author, and perhaps for this very reason people of antiquity who knew the Scriptures best found themselves at a loss to view the Prologue as a skein of human thoughts. Inspired by God? After a few more readings of the Prologue you may want to say you understand how believers could gravitate toward that opinion. But as one who is for the moment interested only in giving the thing an honest human reading, you should not feel in any hurry to share their opinion.

To complete the contrast, take a little time now to read the rest of John's opening chapter. Starting with v. 19, the reader is surrounded by great turbulence: an official investigation, people pulled out of their daily rounds to become disciples, rumors of finding the Messiah, and intimations of awesome scenes to come. Here we have incidents, local disturbances involving local inhabitants, happenings one can become contemporary with. Let us try to illustrate. Read carefully again the closing section, vs. 43–51. What do we move into here as we pick up the exchange between Nathanael and Jesus? What kind of reply is "Rabbi, you are the Son of God! You are the King of Israel"? What would move a skeptical, ironical Israelite to lay divine titles on a fellowman? A hint of the occasion for this is given when Jesus, after greeting Nathanael with a word of praise that startles him, explains by saying he saw Nathanael under the fig tree before Philip found him. Immediately Nathanael responds with the holy titles. Evidently he had not been just walking his dog; something all-out had gone on under the fig tree, something invisible and inaudible to other men, solitary prayer perhaps, but something that tied in with a temptation to deceive. The fact that, humanly speaking, Jesus *could* not have seen him under the fig tree, a haunt chosen by one who took pains to be alone, does not come into the foreground at all but is intimated by Nathanael's astonishment. Are we splicing in fictitious details with no textual evidence to support them? Remember the difference between sheer invention and what is communicated through a character's amazement, exaggerated responses, and the like. This is inference, to be sure, but based on the understanding that you and I are essentially like Nathanael in our ability to tailor our responses to the occasioning circumstances. Nathanael realized he had been observed from afar and his secret thoughts intercepted; this unwritten link assumes its place in the narrative when you read slowly and pause to tighten a loose bulb and see if it lights up.

With few exceptions, turbulence is the earmark of Gospel material, and in these verses it occurs at the level of language, in remarks for which there is no obvious explanation and replies that seem unprepared for. At the heart of his exchange with Jesus is Nathanael's realization that someone at a distance has picked up his most guarded thoughts. *What is it like to discover that I am a transparency to someone, a clear pane of glass that he can see through?* In asking this you would not yet be in conversation with John's Gospel, not yet putting a question to it. Nathanael's discovery is singular; it never comes up in ordinary life, so the possibility is like an unripe fig without much taste. It has to ripen before any taste, sweet or bitter, can trickle down.

One way of letting this possibility ripen is to put down the Gospel and for a few minutes dwell on the fact that you are yourself essentially like Nathanael. Two thousand years and a difference in locale are trifles. Like Nathanael, you have a spot to go to when you want to be alone, for example when your conscience acts up like a bad tooth and insists on some attention. You are tempted, let's say, to misrepresent yourself to someone, maybe on an employment application. To think about this matter you untie the rowboat, as it were, and push out from shore.

Out in the middle of the pond you are isolated. Everything is so still that a dragonfly finds rest on the blade of your shipped oar. Only your thoughts are busy for that quarter of an hour. Finally you think: "What if I don't land that job? It won't be the end of the world."

On the way back to the house you meet a bright-eyed stranger and trade greetings. He knows your name, surprising but not impossible, and tells you his. Then out of the blue he says, "I appreciate someone who can't tolerate lies." It sounds like a compliment, but it is more like an uppercut. How could he know? "Have I met you somewhere?" you manage to ask. "Not exactly," he replies, "but I was watching you through the dragonfly's eye."

Details such as the fig tree or the dragonfly matter little, but meeting someone who can monitor other people's private thoughts would introduce a new factor into your life or mine. Later, when you were out of his sight, you would have to laugh at your sense of relief. It would not take long to realize that you could never achieve any distance from such a one. There is nothing you can keep to yourself any more. At this point natural questions can arise: "Am I not constructed on the same plan as that man? Then why the shattering difference?" And your questions can be ground to a keener edge: "Why would someone capable—don't ask me how—of tuning in other people's thoughts keep surveillance over the minds of ordinary, obscure people? Why not go for the big fish instead of the small fry, emperors instead of nobodies? And if he is not out to undo us, if he has decent intentions, why would he let anyone know of that power, seeing what it does to our peace of mind?"

These questions are not much like Nathanael's glad start. They strike the sour but understandable note of offense or affront. They are akin to Nathanael's joyous response, however, in the sense that they originate in an individual's mentality, not in a school of thought. If the power to intercept secret thoughts and prayers broke into our lives in the form of a fellow human, an equal, its potential for disturbing us on the personal level, whether as a gross invasion of privacy or as the self-announcement of the Messiah, would push into the remote background all concerns that smack of detached scientific investigation. Chilly or offended questions such as "How dare you?" are responses just as personal as Nathanael's, but the reader naturally has to polish them and follow them where they lead. It is up to the Gospel to answer your questions, hot or cold, and to educate you further in the ensuing give-and-take. In fact it is up to the Nazarene himself to answer them, since, as our common idiom goes, he started it. If he tells you obliquely, or in words originally addressed to someone else, why he consorts with sinners and with unimportant people rather than royalty, the particular form his answer takes will not be a disappointment to you, assuming that what you really want is the answer. Sometimes a hint is enough, sometimes a wordless deed tells it all.

The motif of conversation or of "Come, let us reason together" in an individual's reading of Scripture is much more than a figure of speech, as borne out in the first chapter of John. If Nathanael had been praying in secret, exposing his thoughts to God alone, and the newly met stranger acknowledged his prayer, we can begin to understand why the sacred titles forced their way out of Nathanael's throat, and also how an exclamation like "How dare you?" could force itself out of someone else's throat. Of course there is more to conversing. We can spell it out in terms of questions provoked and answered, un-

happy reactions expressed and assuaged, pauses, inter-
ruptions, surprise turns, apparent non sequiturs, ruffled
feelings, mind-searching, inviting, demurring, and numerous other particularities of face-to-face colloquy. Similarly, a phrase like "becoming contemporary with Gospel
events" opens out into descriptions of reading experiences in which the antiquity of the document becomes its
most forgettable feature, the next thing to a disguise. Yet
it would be misleading to view the Gospel as a magical
talking contraption that fires back appropriate sentences
like a live companion. Sometimes it has to be searched,
and the "ancient document" aspect remains an unfading
part of the picture. We could liken a Gospel to an old
settlement that has all the appearances of a ghost town,
where no light comes out of the blackened windows and
the only life in sight is tumbleweeds—but where the doors
are unlocked and where, if you let yourself in, you find
the lights ablaze and plenty of company. The only thing
required to let yourself in is the phrase: "I am essentially
like Nathanael, Philip, the Samaritan woman, Peter, and
the rest."

Looking back briefly, we recall that the majestic, tolling
language of the Prologue to John's Gospel has convinced
many a reader that it was inspired from on high. Argu-
ments for or against that persuasion would be out of place
in a discussion about reading the Bible actively, but a few
unpugnacious remarks might start helpful chains of
thought. First of all, the Prologue is a retrospect, which
means it depends on preexisting Gospel material and ab-
stracts from it. Secondly, the Prologue is the love hymn
of a believer or a family of believers, a hymn to the Word
made flesh, and in that respect it carries a human signa-
ture. When you put these two observations together, the
Prologue does not seem to be intrinsically beyond the pin-
nacles of human literary genius. In contrast, what comes
after the Prologue, namely the Gospel material proper,

seems to this writer to be far above and foreign to every recognized peak of genius in the entire galaxy of letters.

To explain this further, in a Gospel we confront a "literary form" (to use a shamelessly catchall expression) that invites the reader inside for conversations and implicates the reader in what is going on—only not as a reader but as one of the original cast of characters; as one who, like the others, leaves personal fingerprints all over the ancient furniture and glassware. There is a famous mystery novel, Agatha Christie's *The Murder of Roger Ackroyd*, in whose final chapter the finger of blame is pointed at the narrator, but it is several times more mysterious to find a book in which the finger is pointed at the reader, a book that also shatters conventional alibis such as "These events happened long before I was born" or "I was in Florida at the time." No, this "literary form" is something no genius would attempt. A Gospel is not a humanly conceivable project for gifted pens. This, too, is what readers down through the ages have meant by calling the Scriptures inspired.

Faith is not required to make these judgments, as if one could now say for certain, "So you see, it is God's mentality after all that is behind the Gospels." You *see* nothing of the sort. No one even needs to believe in the God of Abraham to be able to say, "I don't know what to make of this. It's like nothing else I've come across."

If it takes divine inspiration to assemble a piece of writing that can act upon and react with the individual reader in the ways described, and in many other ways as well, this will not make the divine activity immediately perceivable. The light it gives off may be dazzling, as for example in Mark 6:45–52, so that a reader needs some time to recover from the glare before the sense of it begins to filter through. Or it may be louvered and diffused, as in the bare image, if that is the right term for it, of the Word becoming flesh; here the central event is presented from an altitude of a weather-watch aircraft flying over the eye of a hurricane. When you look down, all is clear, and the circle of earth below is calm and sunny, with flocks grazing on green slopes and a hush over the treetops. At ground level, however, all around the perimeter of the eye are high winds, thunderheads, torrents, lightning, and funnel clouds.

It is part of the concept "divinely inspired," taken together with the biblical doctrine of a *hidden* God, that inspiration is itself hidden or screened and not publicly obvious, as it would be, for example, if inspired texts glowed in the dark to distinguish themselves from ordinary printed matter. Inspiration can show itself indirectly through the power of a Gospel to interact with the reader so as to disarm any doubts that a hidden but active mentality animates its texts. Spontaneity from the reader's side is needed, too, to keep the conversation going, as some of our examples have shown. Finally, self-critical thinking is required. The New Testament in particular plunges every active reader into a conflict-of-interest situation, and a crisis at that. Our thinking apparently has to come to terms with a troublesome and insistent rumor: the sphere of human affairs has suffered a break-in by a power higher than humanity or nature. With the rumor comes the question that comes separately to each of us: Do I dare look further into this? Do I dare look that rumor in the eye?

For many a reader, especially to someone who has never turned close attention to the Bible until now, the reading experiences we have been discussing point off in the distance to something very different. It is variously called *faith, conversion, becoming a Christian, joining a church,* or other names that suggest a religious turnaround or commitment. Our discussions of reading the Bible break off well short of that kind of step and the type of decision it represents. Insofar as the decision to *read* the Scriptures in a candid, self-involved, conversational way is enormously easier than the religious decision to confess that "Jesus is Lord" and to stick to it, our project remains at all points within the boundaries of the easier decision.

CHAPTER NINE

IN CONCLUSION: THE WORD AS REVEALER

We saw in an earlier chapter that a sinless one entering the human sphere can reveal our situation in an oblique manner, by means of a contrast between ourselves and someone who is on top of human perils. This gives us a handle on the idea that the Bible houses a revelation, but it is impossible to present in summary form a concept such as "revelation" that defines itself over many centuries from Abraham through the apostles. We can derive, for example, from the fright, alarm, and distress of the disciples of Jesus, and from the baffling and numbing effect upon them of the miracles, the reminder that a revelation bears very little resemblance to human wisdom or human deeds. Even at its gentlest, in a healing for instance, it is like a hit from the blind side, a hornet in the shower, something that refuses to be defined or packaged in polite categories. It represents a break-in by that which is most unlike us.

Even though an active reader of a later age can appreciate and actually relive the bruising effects of local turbulence on Nathanael, Peter, and the rest, there is a clear sense in which those happenings are now a matter of record. They have slipped into the past, and a relative stillness has settled over everything. Yet the Bible presents to later arrivals like you and me a kind of calling card that is basically the same as what the disciples received. Its message, or rather its overture, is that the power behind the turbulence *knows* you and me, that he is wise to every wrinkle of our being. There are texts to this effect, such as John 2:23–25:

> Now when he was in Jerusalem at the Passover feast, many believed in his name when they saw the signs which he did; but Jesus did not trust himself to them, because he knew all men and needed no one to bear witness of man; for he himself knew what was in man.

It is a text that can drift across a reader's line of sight without attracting much notice, but let us take a minute to ask: Do I know what is in me? Do you know what is in you?

As we approach a sampling of what the Bible declares to be in us, let us use the not very revealing name "God" for the mentality behind the Bible. If there is a divine revelation housed in that book, then God knows that inheriting it, as you and I have done, is somewhat like inheriting the Amazon Basin, where it is a good deal easier to get lost than to strike it rich. He is aware, too, of how outrageous some of the biblical claims about us must sound to someone brought up with twentieth-century habits of thought, and he will not expect someone with those habits to give ground without a struggle. In revealing you to yourself in your often unsuspected sides and depths, God reveals himself initially as a power that invites you to share his knowledge of you, a power that would make you free from lies and illusions.

If the Bible contains a divine revelation, then, it will reveal you to yourself in ways that human analysis could never bring to light. Among the things it claims to know is that you hunger for eternal life but do not know how to lay hold of it (Luke 18:18–23). Are these claims accurate?

Can you own up to them personally? They are at any rate the kind of claim that you can test out by exploring trails, familiar and otherwise, within yourself. If you have not given much direct thought to matters eternal, then you run up against another biblical overture: you lack the truth about yourself and the freedom that goes with it (John 8:31–38). Here someone might react: "It is a little strange to be told that I lack truth, since I make my way about quite capably from day to day. Over the years I have formed a set of workable opinions about my existence, some candid and honest beliefs about what my priorities ought to be. If I lack truth, this can only mean I have fallen for some untruths about myself, and I do not take kindly to that suggestion. Not only is it insulting but it sounds like a lot of malarkey."

Your back talk shows that the biblical overture has touched a nerve, challenging your basic, habitual way of looking at your existence. This is an occasion to look afresh at bottom-line judgments about your life and its purpose and direction. If the Bible is spouting malarkey at you, it is at least the kind of malarkey that you can run a check on. You can take a new look at what you really think of yourself, at what you take to be your best feature or the most important thing about you, and see if you can detect anything fishy about your bedrock convictions, now that you have heard them challenged.

If God is aware of how alien his biblical overtures must sound to people like ourselves, he makes no effort to tone them down. Their foreignness can also be a clue to the distance they crossed to reach you. For example, the Bible keeps echoing the theme that you and I, creatures of the late twentieth century, are implicated in the human race at large, not merely by belonging to one of its generations but also by sharing with Adam in its primordial downfall and need for redemption. How alien this sounds! What could be more farfetched? Here a spark of indignation might touch off a first response like this: "Why, the case would be thrown out of any earthly court! Don't I as a human being come into the world with a clean slate, even if my great-grandfather happened to be a horse thief or whatever?" Back talk is a familiar element in conversation, and it can serve as a spur to investigate yourself with regard to those surprising specifics which the Bible lays at your doorstep. The ones we have noted are easy to summarize:

1. You lack the truth about yourself and its attendant freedom.
2. You are attached to some untrue convictions about yourself.
3. You hunger for unending happiness but lack the key to it.
4. You have an infinite side to your nature that implicates you in human history long past and in eternity to come.

These are arresting claims. They do not state the obvious. To the extent that the Bible can make them stick, they illustrate part of what it means for God to reveal himself indirectly by revealing you to yourself.

The books of Scripture contain a good many more claims than the four just listed, many of them mindnumbing and defiant of immediate understanding. Our small selection, however, is enough to show that the overall intent of the biblical material is to free you and me from the grip of untruths, illusions, and myths about ourselves, some of which have become second nature to us so that it scarcely occurs to anyone to question them. Instead of shattering our habits of thought with a power play, or purging our untruths by an unthinkable display of majesty, the mind behind the Bible chooses to act from hiddenness, playing a waiting game behind its ghost-town facade. It does not try to appear chic, modern, relevant, or revolutionary, but waits for a knock from someone who longs for nothing else than to be free of manmade illusions. It does not force its knowledge on you but puts it before you unspectacularly, in simple language, as if to ask how seriously you yearn for truth and freedom. If you are serious about that, your task is to go on and see if the Scriptures can develop their overtures in a convincing manner, for it would be odd if they convinced you or anyone else at first sight.

Just at this point a question is likely to form in the reader's mind: "Is there not an obstacle in the Bible's extraordinary way of perceiving us? It sees you and me as destitute, cleaving to lies about ourselves, dogged by obscure hungers, and, though we are recent arrivals, trailing silken strands that tie us back to the origins of humanity and tug us forward in time as well. Don't we have a different, more up-to-date way of perceiving ourselves? Is it not in large part *scientific*? And doesn't it claim to have analyzed our origin, nature, and destiny right down to the behavior of molecules?"

It is a fair question. If God keeps under lock and key his power to dazzle us with grandeur, what power is left to him? Even if the Scriptures are his Word, what sort of power can the Word exert that can trump the modern scientific vision of life?

In a nutshell, the Word has the power to get personal with you by revealing you to yourself. If you are an active reader, the biblical texts have the power to speak to your personal mentality, to quicken it, to spring surprises, to expose and terminate illusions. In earlier discussions we saw how variously the texts function. Genesis, for example, reinforced by psalms and other texts, implants a concept of God and a concept of humanity, shaping the contours of our thought and language, yet letting us be ourselves. Elsewhere a sinless one reveals our situation through a contrast with his own, and shakes to its foundations our whole modern notion of the "naturalness" of death. In another instance a Gospel story lets you slip into the ancient scenery and share Peter's grieving wait at the lake's edge. What you have in common with someone in Palestine in Roman times becomes a passkey, enabling you to probe your own response to Nathanael's experience when the newfound Messiah gets personal with him. There is much more, of course. All these moments exhibit the Bible's power to draw from each of us responses that in many instances can lead to sustained conversation. Because it takes two, the Word functions by enlisting you yourself in the project of self-discovery, which is at the same time a revealer of God.

These remarks will be incomplete unless we add: a scientific theory cannot reveal you to yourself. Let us be quite specific about this by addressing a theory that everyone has heard at least a little about. When one of the most eminent spokesmen for human evolution writes, "Man is a biological species which has evolved from ancestors who were not men" (T. Dobzhansky, *The Biological Basis of Human Freedom*, p. 9), it is natural to suppose that the term "man" refers to you, me, and Dobzhansky, among millions of others. It is natural also to suppose that the author means to reveal something unexpected and startling about your origins, namely that nonhuman ancestors occur somewhere back in your family tree. Dobzhansky is only repeating the main conclusion of Darwin's *The Descent of Man* (1871), which states that man is descended from some lowly organized form.

Undoubtedly many a person has been disconcerted by the central thesis of human evolution, sensing correctly that it somehow deeply alters an older, even a prebiblical, concept of ourselves. Certainly no other idea in the past century has shown such a vast potential for spreading confusion. A little careful thought, however, will spare you from being misled by that central thesis. In the first

place you know from your own history that *you* did not
come into existence by evolving from nonhumans, nor
have you ever met anyone who did. The thesis, though it
speaks of "man," lacks any application to yourself or any
individual you know, and if you think further about this,
you will quickly realize that it does not apply to any man,
woman, or child who ever existed. But if the term "man"
in those sentences of Darwin and Dobzhansky does not
apply to you or me or any other human being, then *what*
are they saying descended from nonhuman stocks? The
whole literature of human evolution leaves this question
up in the air. When someone challenges the central thesis, the commonest line of reply is to concede that you and
I did not evolve or descend from brute ancestors, but that
man understood as *the human species* did. This reply has
gotten many a pleader for human evolution off the hook,
for few people have the patience for a seesawing debate
over whether humankind is a species or something else.
However, if you stand your ground just a little longer and
ask what exactly is meant by the term "the human species," you will discover that even the most accomplished
speaker takes refuge in vague references to "biological
man," "the human type," "the human form," "the common gene pool," and similar abstractions, all of which
stand in very questionable relation to a "man" or a
"woman" in the sense of ourselves and other flesh-and-
blood humans. The result is that it never becomes clear
what is alleged to have descended from those shadowy ancestors, although admittedly you and I did not. The key
Darwinian thesis concerning human origins remains as
hopelessly murky today as on the day it was published.

Our main point would stand even if (inconceivably)
someone came along to give a clear sense to Darwin's key
thesis. That is, a scientific theory cannot reveal you to
yourself, for the theorist knows you only as a type,
through what you have in common with others of the

same type, for instance a standard set of human bones, organs, and tissues. The researcher does not know you as an original and unique personality, or in the depths of your privacy. That originality and those depths are precisely what the mind behind the Bible searches out, penetrates, and reveals to you. You need only think back to the first chapters of Genesis to recall that the Bible presents human beings as the supreme creation, each one profoundly original. The New Testament in turn gives out that each human masterwork is worth saving for eternity. If you do not think of yourself as a masterwork, or as profoundly original, or as made in the image of God, the biblical reply is that you do not yet know yourself. The mind behind the Scriptures is aware that it is not saying the obvious and that you and I may very well need some convincing about the treasures bound up with an average human life, since various illusions and untruths can stand in the way of our appreciating that gift. You may in fact see no good reason to start off by believing these things about yourself. The source of the Word, however, is prepared to do the necessary convincing and to dissolve the individual's illusions, using the power of the Word itself. Paul describes that power in vivid if sometimes puzzling images in Heb. 4:12:

> For the word of God is living and active, sharper than any two-edged sword, piercing to the division of soul and spirit, of joints and marrow, and discerning the thoughts and intentions of the heart.

In order for the Word to help reveal you to yourself, the first imperative is to hold fast to your individual mentality, for that is part of your native equipment. It is also the part that the Scriptures are addressed to: the mind, the understanding, and the limitations as well, of a single human being who is subject to vexation, unclearness, uncertainty, bafflement, and surprises. It is the mentality of someone who may not know much about DNA or quarks but is totally convinced that he or she is not a team, a corporation, or a school of thought. Such a person carries no top-heavy superstructure of convictions of the sort we associate with this or that dedicated group. Consequently no dismantling needs to be done before this individual is ready to sit down for some informal talk.

When we speak of the power of the biblical Word to release you from illusions and reveal you to yourself, we should also take note of forces in our society that propagate illusions. The idea of human evolution, which has its own brass band as noted earlier, is tied in with a broader cosmic picture that has made itself part of everybody's compulsory education. In that picture every natural phenomenon is presumed to be explainable as the product of mindless laws of nature. Beauty, too, in the abstract art of a moth's wing, a feather, the bright eyes of a salamander, and in your children's faces—yes, beauty too is explained as nature churns out her replicas in robotic obedience to the genetic code of each species. This picture gives off a sooty fallout that can dull everything, including our ability to read the Bible profitably. The illusion is that we completely understand natural phenomena, or at least that science does—from the last ladybug to the baby who is due next month.

The penetrating antidote to this lazy habit of modern thought is to salute *new* beings for what they are. Even people acquainted with the Scriptures can become habituated to the idea that Creation has to do with only the first stages of the universe, the eons in which God laid the foundations, using durable materials, and revved up all the basic mechanisms, living and inanimate, to perform the same kinds of operation again and again. And now, having learned her laws, we *understand* nature. Go up for a close look at whatever is about to flower around your home. Maybe you remember from last spring seeing little bunched fists of unbloomed lilac getting ready to open next day. Look at whatever is poking through the soil and say to yourself: "These are *new*. These never existed before this week. And in 1938 *I* was spanking new, and twenty-odd years later my daughter was new, and a few years after that my son. We were each in turn as new as these dogtooth violets." Newness is a scriptural motif through both Testaments, and at the core of the biblical meaning of Creation is the idea that Creation is still going on. It wouldn't hurt us at all to paste on office walls and refrigerator doors the ancient verse: "This is the day which the LORD has made" (Ps. 118:24). We are taught in school, with models and diagrams, that the whirling of the earth produces days and nights in unending succession, and this is probably how things appear to the corporate mentality of science, which is so fond of the big picture and the mechanical explanation. To our pint-sized human mentalities, on the other hand, a day is something you wake up to. Today is as new as the violet that wasn't there yesterday. The corporate mind, not bound to a living body, never sleeps, so it never really wakes up either.

Can you or I fully understand the coming into existence of a new life? The drift of the Bible seems to be negative on this question.

> From thy lofty abode thou waterest the moun-
>   tains;
> the earth is satisfied with the fruit of thy
>   work.
> Thou dost cause the grass to grow for the cattle,
>   and plants for man to cultivate,
> that he may bring forth food from the earth,
>   and wine to gladden the heart of man,

oil to make his face shine,
and bread to strengthen man's heart.
(Ps. 104:13–15)

An engineer can understand every detail of a process for manufacturing a complex apparatus, but the appearance of a new plant or animal or baby leaves a shortfall of understanding in an individual human mind. The unknown is a factor, for even when the seed corn is planted under the best of conditions, the dirt farmer and the professor of agronomy alike have to wait and see what comes up, and this puts a dash of the mysterious into every new leaf and blade. The farmer knows what conditions he must provide in order to get a crop, and the agronomist knows these conditions in much finer detail, but neither one can know that these constitute *all* the conditions for generating new plants. If Creation is still with us, one of those conditions is hidden.

Explicitly you and I are told that we are distinct and once-only creations, not retreads or replicas but recent arrivals. "Remember also your Creator in the days of your youth" (Eccl. 12:1). Inexhaustibly, then, Creation keeps coming at us. How, though, can I train myself to perceive the new *as* new and not as a weary cyclical repetition? For that purpose I must never let go of my small personal mentality, or merge it so completely with a corporate one that it can no longer raise a shout of welcome to the first grape hyacinths of the season.

The power of the biblical Word to get personal with you, and gradually to reveal and share with you its intimate knowledge of your inmost being, simply outranks the various disciplines we lump together under the name of science. Those are human disciplines, and it does them no dishonor to add that their histories are marked by frailty, nearsightedness, exaggeration, oversimplification, pretense, and illusions—along with, of course, numerous triumphs. In contrast, it is not a human prerogative to reveal an individual to himself or herself in depths the human eye cannot reach, to expose and dispel the untruths and illusions that collect within, and finally to heal the places they once infested. There have been great human teachers and physicians, as everyone will admit, but here we escalate far above the concept of a reliable preceptor or medical man and move toward the concept of Creator and Redeemer.

As a parting word, if the Bible contains a revelation (and why should you take anyone's word for that?), then it is quite capable of doing for you the things here described, and much besides. It will not need help from other books to prove that it contains a revelation. It will prove that by revealing. It also offers promises of eternal life and joy, the portal to which is faith. Having said once or twice already that, as between reading the Bible and living in faith, the first is vastly easier than the second, I must leave the harder topic to those more practiced in it.

REFERENCES

In this volume reference is made to the following books, which are listed here alphabetically.

Chesterton, G. K. *The Everlasting Man.* Doubleday & Co., Image Books, 1955.

Christie, Agatha. *The Murder of Roger Ackroyd.* Triangle Books, 1943.

Darwin, Charles. *The Descent of Man.* D. Appleton & Co., 1871.

Derrett, John D. M. *Law in the New Testament.* London: Darton, Longman & Todd, 1970.

Dobzhansky, T. G. *The Biological Basis of Human Freedom.* Columbia University Press, 1956.

Kierkegaard, Søren. *Søren Kierkegaard's Journals and Papers.* Edited & translated by Howard V. Hong and Edna H. Hong. Vol. I. Indiana University Press, 1967.